The Path of Mankind

The Journey From Created To Creator

A Dictation From The Great White Brotherhood

Bob Sanders

DISCLAIMERS

This is a free eBook. You are free to give it away (in unmodified form) to whomever you wish. If you have paid for this eBook you should request or seek an immediate refund.

The author has made every effort to ensure the accuracy of the information within this book was correct at time of publication. The author does not assume and hereby disclaims any liability to any party for any loss, damage, or disruption caused by errors or omissions, whether such errors or omissions result from accident, negligence, or any other cause.

COPYRIGHT

This book was authored by Bob Sanders and messaged to him from The Great White Brotherhood by clairaudience, or as some people call "channelling". It is free for everyone to read and share for spiritual advancement.

Please share this book with anyone and anywhere you can to help spread the messages it contains.

For more information please visit the following internet sites:

http://www.thegreatwhitebrotherhood.org

http://www.thestairwaytofreedom.org

https://www.youtube.com/channel/UC2UDv0r4mtNPEWbve5YHDeg/

First edition – October 2017

Cover Artwork by Paul Saunders

I.S.B.N. – 9781973278559
Author – Bob Sanders

TABLE OF CONTENTS

FOREWORD

Chapter 1 - THE GREAT DESIGN

Chapter 2 - THE GREAT DIVIDE

Chapter 3 - THE ILLUMINATION OF MAN

Chapter 4 - THE WAY TOWARDS FREEDOM

Chapter 5 - LIFE IN LIGHT

Chapter 6 - MOVING HOUSE

Chapter 7 - INTO THE KNOWN

Chapter 8 - THE HARD LIFE

Chapter 9 - THE DYING PROCESS

Chapter 10 - INTO THE LIGHT

Chapter 11 - THE WAY THROUGH THE LIGHT

FOREWORD

The field of esoteric knowledge is vast and complex. Its effect on humanity has been accepted and rejected by groups of people over eons of time because humanity has been present on Earth and in the esoteric planes of reality for a long time.

The impression given by science, religion and archaeology as to the presence of humanity on Earth is a long way from the truth as groups came and went over periods of time.

Man has recently started to investigate and discover elements suggesting that history has not accurately recorded the occupation of man's home planet but only evidence of recent occupation remains.

Time has eliminated all trace of the earlier sojourns made by man upon the planet so it is not possible for science to trace the beginning of humanity's origins.

That is not to say that no record remains but it does indicate that it will not be possible to discover archaeological evidence remaining.
To trace the origins of man's beginnings we must look elsewhere.

This new book, investigating the makeup of mankind is intended to probe elements of total man from his earliest beginnings up to the present time in as complete a fashion as is possible, leaving no stone unturned in our efforts to grasp just who and what this creature called man is and his place in the overall concept of life.

It is intended that this volume should take man on into the future by examining minutely his past origins both in physical and non-physical forms.

By doing so, it is hoped that when considered in conjunction with the previous work presented (The Stairway To Freedom), it will be both complementary and innovative and thus form a comprehensive work that will explain the origins of man, his place in the universe and his destiny ultimately throughout the stars for, be assured that man came from the stars and his place, his destiny, is to return.

Man is a far greater creature than history has portrayed.
Most of what has been written to explain his origins is incorrect either by ignorance of the facts or by falsehood.

This volume, in conjunction with the previous, sets out to correct these errors and anyone who takes the effort to read and understand them will no longer be under the illusion as to his origins, his path through life and his future as he progresses through the maze of intricacies of life in his attempt to return to his source - God.

So, it must, at the outset, be fully understood by all that this proposed volume will be both diverse and complex in its investigations of life and so the student must be prepared, both in the sense of understanding of the task being undertaking and also by preparation for comprehension of its elements, by prior study.

This will not be a work understandable by all and, indeed, no one who has not armed himself by previous investigation should undertake its study.

However, for those who have prepared themselves correctly and for those who will make the effort of deep analysis of the topics to be mentioned it is hoped that clarity will be afforded and strides made to remove the barriers that have for so long been erected to keep the truth from the eyes of the searchers.

This day was bound to come.

Truth can only be hidden for so long.

It was kept from the curious public for long ages for a variety of reasons but times change and the changing time has decreed that now is the moment for unveiling the evidence that has been waiting to be presented.

So, with these admonishments as to the degree of preparation required and the level of comprehension expected, we will now start to begin to explain both the physical and spiritual origins of man from the dawns of time and into his probable future.

CHAPTER ONE

THE GREAT DESIGN

People have long wondered about the origin of humanity, where it came from and why.

It appears that all other life is so simple and trouble free. Mammals, fish and all the creatures that inhabit Earth seem to get by worry free. They do not need clothes, they all seem to find enough to eat each day and, when they have nothing better to do, they sleep, deep, untroubled sleep until they feel that it is the moment to wake up and pursue some other activity; hunting, mating, eating and, once that craving satisfied, they sleep again.

The only variation to this pattern seems to occur when an animal has young to care for. Then, and only then, does another instinct come to the fore that we term "the maternal instinct".

Then the selfish aspects that dominates most of their lives takes a back seat and, for the first time, the creature, or creatures, start to put others first and themselves second or not at all.

Many creatures will give their lives and die, if necessary, protecting their young if attacked by a predator intent on harming those young.

For the first time we see in such creatures' instincts that we could recognise and approve of.

We sometimes give these attributes human characteristics and talk of "motherly love", and the "maternal instinct" of such animals.

Whether the animals themselves would recognise such attributes or whether they are merely following the instincts that nature has instilled in them is another matter.

But, from our point of view we can associate with the actions of a female mammal suckling its cuddly young and lavishing upon them as much care as even the most attentive human could.

This connection between the way in which an animal cares for its young and the attitude that decent humans have towards each other provides a clue as to the difference and the similarity between the animal population and humans.

So we can see that humans clearly have, in certain circumstances, attributes, both that we call positive and negative, a connection between the animal kingdom and us.

It is possible for man to be completely callous, selfish and looking out exclusively for himself but it is possible for man to be loving, caring, laying down his life to save another if required.

Thus we can clearly see the connection in animalistic terms between man and beast.

Yet for most thinking people it is clear that man is not an animal.

Animals do not wear clothes but man does.

Animals seem, generally, to be able to provide their nourishment for themselves where as man, in the same circumstances would have to ape animal behaviour and hunt or grub in the dirt for food or succumb to starvation.

He would not be able to have the types of food that he is used to in civilised society.

One could go on. Even hive creatures like ants and bees live by different rules to man, even though their behaviour has been long admired by some people and attempts to install such a hierarchical system of control, from one almighty being (the queen ant or bee) down through a military type of protection system, to the workers, toiling endlessly without question to provide all that the hive or nest requires, their useless bodies, once they have expired through exhaustion, either being recycled as food for the living or being ejected outside the nest as useless dross.

Such a system would gain great popularity in many communities but can hardly be approved when compared to the love given by a mother animal to its offspring.

So where does this comparison of the different aspects of animal life take us. Does it help in any way or fashion to discover the origins of mankind?

We have looked at some of the aspects of animalistic behaviour and considered the cold, almost military way that certain insect groups behave, through the "normal" somewhat selfish mindset of the average animal and then considered the loving, caring, giving aspects of certain creatures during the period where they have young to care for.

Now let us go back a long way in time before anything that we would describe as living existed.

What did the world look like?

It is possible to conjecture that, if one trawls far enough back in time, we would arrive at a point where nothing existed.

Such an exercise would provide little edification in identifying the origin of the creation of man, so we skip forward to the point where planets exist but life on them does not.

It is not possible to put a precise date on such a period because, due to the fact that life as we know it did not exist, no one was present to measure or note such a time!

And yet something must have existed in order to organise and put in motion the wheels of creation that have resulted in all that we currently see.

If we are to find out what that "something" was that kick-started life, perhaps, by extrapolation, we can uncover the source from whence mankind appeared.

So, we are at a point where planets now exist but there is no life as we would know it anywhere in the universe.

This is where we need to move outside of physicality and grope the depths of the invisible worlds, real and vibrant within their own dimensions but only recently thought about by a branch of science known as quantum mechanics.

This branch of investigation of life, unfortunately, describes these different universes as bands, strings, lifeless mathematical concepts that may, indeed, describe the basic concept of the various dimensions but fails, totally, to embrace the reality of the dynamic essence that these dimensions actually portray.

Indeed, it is true to say that, without the various dimensions that science has only recently discovered, physical reality would not be possible because, what is visible around us that is called reality is the end result of the complex interplay of the dimensional forces that permit so called reality to exist as has been explained in previous works.

So we need to discover how and why dimensions came into being before we can hope, eventually, to discover how man could have physical form on planet Earth.

Life is very complex and yet life is the only thing that exists.

Where did this life come from?

This is where we have to admit that we have a gap in our knowledge.

Many of us have spent vast amounts of time and energy investigating this mysterious force but it seems to be deemed to be the one great unsolvable mystery.

We feel the need to explain somewhat but the conundrum can be summed up in the question that has been asked for millennia; What came first, the chicken or the egg?

If and when anyone can satisfactorily answer that question, he will have the key to the question of where life came from.

Obviously, over time, wise men have pondered the question and have proposed some very intelligent solutions but none of them have stood the test of time.

The chicken and egg mystery is, of course, closely connected to another; who created everything in the first place?

Science, generally, ignores such questions, preferring to deal with subjects to which they can provide answers.

Religions claim the monopoly of knowledge as to who and what God is but, if pushed, will have to admit that the origin of God is a mystery to them.

As far as is known, the origin of the life force known as God, is not understood by any force anywhere in the various galaxies nor in the dimensions enrobing the galaxies.

So, there is this one, vital point that, for the moment, remains unanswerable. Perhaps it is just as well because if it was discovered that the life force we call God was "made" by some other life force, we would open a Pandora's box of questions as to who invented who indefinitely.

We are looking for answers, not endless questions so we start with the premise that states that some force, that some people refer to as God, is a life force and is the only life force that has ever existed or ever will.

Nothing can exist in any plane of reality, from physical to the uppermost dimension, unless it has this life force associated with it.

It may be difficult to comprehend that a grain of sand is alive but it is so.

Now we should, perhaps, elucidate at this point that being alive does not necessarily imply sentience or to have the ability to move.

Life comes in many forms. Some are totally static and apparently lifeless such as rocks and stones and others are capable of moving at speed, such as birds. But they all contain one thing - life.

So what is life?

We will not insult your intelligence by describing the physical events observable on Earth.

We are interested in examining the life force, invisible, behind and beyond anything that can be measured by instruments connected to a sick person in an hospital to indicate to the hospital staff that the physical body of the patient still has a beating heart.

The life force is an invisible, unknowable energy that was mentioned earlier that was referred to as God.

As we do not know what God is, except for the fact that it contains the life force, so we cannot actually explain what that life force is.

But we do know one important aspect of it.

There is but one life force!

To many people alive on Earth today this fact is known but there are also large numbers of people both incarnate and discarnate who do not know this fundamental truth.

All life is one.

Ridiculous as this seems, it is true.

Accepting this fact has enabled us to look back in time to the point that was mentioned earlier in this chapter, the place where planets existed but there was no life on any of the planets nor in any of the dimensions that were also mentioned.

So we have to accept that this life force created, using the laws of physics, a variety of planets in an invisible series of vibrational constructs that we refer to as dimensions.

Each dimension can be imagined as a planet or series of planets, real and solid but each dimension separated from another due to being subject to a different carrier wave.

It appears that the mysterious life force we call God created these dimensions as different experiments in its quest to discover just what life would create, because life is not just a static force, it contains curiosity, desire for knowledge, for expansion and so, to assist it in its quest for self awareness and growth, different bands of vibrations were set up and, by the law of mutual attraction - a fundamental part of the law of God - planets corresponding to that particular vibration were created.

This force we call God set up eight distinct bands, dimensions and furnished these dimensions with planets.

Now, we have to appreciate that God, this life force; is one unique life force. This being so it could only create one life.

But in order to create a maximum of opportunity for expansion and knowledge (wisdom), it divided this one life force into eight subsections by altering, dividing, the one life force into eight different vibratory bands.

We wish you to comprehend that all around you is the universe that you can observe in the night sky, and much more outside of the milky way, repeated another seven times, each universe identical to the one you observe but invisible to your eyes because it is subject to a carrier wave of a slightly different frequency.

The universe in which you currently live is also vibrating but you are not aware of it as you, yourself, are part of this effect and vibrate in harmony with your visible universe.

You also have bodies that are part and parcel of the other universes but we will deal with that subject later.

So, to labor the point, we wish to make it clear to you that this force we call God, which is life, and life contains intelligence, created what you refer to as a physical universe but also created seven more universes on different carrier waves - copies of the physical universe.

However, the total of all eight universes are one and that one we refer to as God.

So the form of man is multi layered, multi dimensional that, together, make the person we know as man.

This fact has been kept from humanity for long ages because a control system that was constructed also long ages ago for the simple reason to keep mankind enslaved, under servitude to a relatively few people who, themselves, may not know the truth about man but have been educated to act as controllers of humanity.

We need to examine who these controllers, these overseers of humanity are and why they do this.

To understand this slave system will take us outside of physicality and into at least one of the dimensions.

Everything that we see in the physical world, as was stated, is multi dimensional.

Everything physical has eight layers. The physical reality is the lowest but man, just to concentrate on him, has seven other layers or bodies each one separated from his physical body, and his other bodies, by a different carrier wave frequency.

So, to reiterate, man is a creature with eight different but identical bodies, each one standing in a universe but each one enwrapped in that unique universe due to being encoded by a different unique frequency.

However, not all life forms are quite like that. Some, like man when he "dies", discards the lowest frequency and moves his consciousness into the next, higher, frequency and finds himself alive and present in that frequency.

The more higher frequencies are present but, because he is not aware that he has these other bodies, he does not explore them and so they remain quiescent, awaiting the happy day when he does become aware of them and decides to explore them with his mind.

But there are many entities that do not have physicality. They may well have all the other higher auras, as they are called, and some of them have developed the ability to move into them at will and explore the wonders that are available in those worlds.

Equally, there are other beings that live in the esoteric realms that are so cut off from the God force that their higher frequencies are virtually non-existent.

One such group have been known of for long ages and have been given the name "The Archons". These creatures live in a dimension just outside of the physical dimension and, as was stated, because they have chosen to ignore their higher frequencies, are totally cut off from any positive power that automatically flows from the higher realms into the lower.

Thus, these beings, the Archons, have all of their consciousness concentrated in this one etheric band, all else, in effect, not existing as far as they are concerned.

Now, these entities, the Archons, are totally unaware and totally, non-affected by any thoughts and feelings of their higher concepts.

Nothing that we would consider holy or Godlike enters their minds or their realities.

But these creatures are real, thinking beings although, if we were to meet one and try to converse with it, we would find their thoughts so "alien" to ours that it would be quite impossible to find any common ground for dialogue.

They, like all life, have existed for a very long time but have made no progress towards the Godhead, which is the prime consideration of the majority of life.

Thus, they are unique, outcasts from all other life, containing, not evil as such, but total non-consideration for anything or anyone outside of themselves.

However, like all things, they are immortal.

Virtually all other life progresses slowly from one frequency to another, discarding the lower frequencies as they do, rather like peeling the layers from an onion until, finally, they reveal their goal - the Godhead.

Although, with all life, it takes an enormous amount of time to move to that final vibration - the Godhead - all creatures are aware, at some level, that the frequency exists and so all creatures, whatever their shape, form or origin retain a sense of holiness, albeit, in some creatures, closely hidden from their actual level but, nevertheless, it is there and guides all life upwards from frequency to frequency, carrier wave to carrier wave, the lower ones being cast off as they rise.

All life does this except one group - the Archons.

They have remained static for so long that they cannot imagine that anything else exists, any higher form of life exists.

This, over eons of time has moulded a particular character both in an individual sense and in a collective regard.

Thus, they would, from our perspective, seem to be very one sided. Totally focussed on the very things that the majority of us try to reject; fear, hate, jealousy and all the things that we consider negative and make us unhappy.

Thus, most of us seek to live in situations where these emotions are not uppermost in our lives and we try to replace them with love and friendliness.

But these unfortunate beings, the Archons, know only these negative emotions.

Indeed, if someone spoke to one of these Archons and suggested that there were other, better emotions that he could include in his makeup, he would think we were mad.

Nothing that could be considered positive by us would enter the mind of the Archonic creatures and so they live in a world of hate.

A dark world, indeed!

So, to make things clear. These Archons are not aware of any frequencies higher than the one in which they live but, a long time ago, they became aware of a frequency beneath theirs.

This, unfortunately, is the one that physical life lives in. Your world!

The aim of all life is to move in frequency. With the vast majority of life, the movement takes them upwards in frequency into the higher, more holy frequencies.

In the case of the Archons, they, too, feel the need to explore other frequencies and progress into them if they can. But, as they are totally unaware that higher realms exist, this drive took them to explore the only frequency they could which happens to be the physical realm.

It must be remembered that Archons are non-physical and so they don't have physical bodies. Thus, they found it impossible actually to integrate this lower frequency into their creation. They remain etheric beings.

However, the drive to move in frequency is paramount in all life and the Archons are no exception.

Many long years ago they found that they could, in certain circumstances, integrate your world somewhat, not in a physical sense but by taking over the minds of humans.

However, they hit a snag, a problem that they could not deal with.

As they tried to integrate with humans, they found that the minds of most humans, even those long years ago, contained elements of the higher, more holy frequencies.

This was incompatible with their frequency and so they found that they could not mould with the majority of humans.

However, the drive to change frequency being irresistible, they looked for a way to resolve the problem and find a group of people with whom they could integrate, people like minded with them, totally concentrated on self with none of the higher emotions present in their personalities.

Long years ago they discovered a group that thought like them. This group we consider to be victims of an illness that causes them to be unlike most of us. The majority of people are naturally gentle, kind, loving and generous, putting others - if not first in their lives - at least more or less equal to them and worthy of consideration.

However, there is this relatively small group of people who do not think like the majority.

This group only think of themselves, their needs, wants and ambitions and are willing to do anything to satisfy their aims.

We call them psychopaths.

This was the very group that the Archons were searching for, people like minded with them and so they found it easy to mould with these people, integrate their personalities and, virtually, to become one with them.

However, these psychopathic people found themselves outcasts from most societies, either banished, imprisoned or executed.

This did not serve the Archonic needs. There was no point in integrating with a person only to find that person banished, imprisoned or to have his physical incarnation terminated.

So the solution was found.

It was decided to put these people above the law and the system of making them rulers was introduced.

Further, over time, it was found that not all psychopaths could be made into kings or queens, so other systems were set up placing as many Archon influenced people in positions of power and authority, the idea being that they were placed in situations where the Archon influence for various forms of negativity could be exercised but the people being influenced were above the law, untouchable by any person not thinking as they did.

So, over many generations in virtually all countries of the world, the psychopathic people are in the top positions, outside of any control by other, more noble people.

All this was kept strictly secret from the public who, if they had been informed of what was going on, would have taken steps to remedy the situation.

So this is the sad state that the physical world and the physical situation is in.

This book is, in part, intended to be an alarm call, a wake-up call of what is going on.

Now, it must be explained that not all people in power are Archon controlled psychopaths but it must be realised that many, indeed most, are.

However, nothing lasts forever. The only constant is change and change is, at last, occurring both in the physical part of planet Earth and, more importantly, in the etheric and spiritual dimensions.

This change takes the form of an energetic wave rising that will, eventually, wake people up to realise their spiritual makeup as they start to make contact with their higher vibrational bodies and take steps to eliminate from power these Archonic driven souls who have been causing so much harm for so long.

However, the Archons, like so many psychopaths have as their base drive, fear. They are constantly on the look out for attack.

God loving people do not require fear as a dominant part of their personalities as they instinctively know that they are part of the God force and God is love. If the love given by God is an integral part of the personality of virtually all people - having been made by this force we call God - fear has very little hold over them, even those who pretend that God does not exist. So love for all humanity is present in the makeup of most people, with the exception of the psychopaths and, more importantly, the psychopaths under the domination of the Archons.

With this group, fear is their dominant motive and controls most of their actions. They are constantly on the lookout for any force, any action, by any person or group that could attack them and reduce their control.

So they take whatever actions they can to prevent anything from happening that could affect them in any way.

This fear of attack manifests itself in many ways. They ban people from demonstrating for peace if they can. They fill the leisure moments of many people with various entertainments; sport, TV, cinema and so on that keeps the people from thinking. They fill the entertainment areas with as much violence as they can in the desire to keep the public in a state of negativity so that the actions of the leaders are not far removed from the actions portrayed in so called entertainment.

Thus there is much importance placed on sports; boxing, football, rugby, swimming, running and all the various athletic sports, all designed to be competitive and all designed to keep people in fear in case their sportsman, their team, fails to win.

The television is full of films of violence and programs of the harmful things going on in the world, all designed to generate fear.

The financial situation it designed to create fear in case there is not sufficient money earned to survive.

All this has been carefully designed for two reasons:

To promote fear which is Archonic in nature.

To make the public as much like the leaders as possible so that they do not see what the leaders are doing as the thoughts of the public are similar to the thoughts of the psychopaths that are in power.

These Archon controlled psychopaths understand that if the public realised their God force and turned to it, they would see through what has been constructed by the Archons and would remove their minions, your leaders, from power.

This day, fortunately, will come.

It is time.

The reason why it is time will be discussed in a later chapter but, rest assured, that the time has come.

Now, it has been suggested by many that the Archons use fear as food. This is not strictly true. Non-physical beings do not require sustenance. However, it is also true that all energy expended must be replaced from somewhere.

Physical people eat to sustain physical life.

Astral beings naturally draw sustenance from the God force that is everywhere.

However, the Archons, being negative, have cut themselves off from the God force, so that cannot sustain them.

Therefore, they do use fear, generated by their actions, as a sort of sustenance. It has actually very little regenerative power compared to the God force but it is all they have.

It must be realised that, being non-physical, they cannot die but they can grow weak.

In the past they managed, through wars, slavery and serf systems, heartless religions and so on to create a lot of fear which sustained them but nowadays, even wars create less fear as there is very little hand to hand combat which was a source of generating actual terror.

So the latest thing that has been invented is terrorism; terror - ism.

We could go on.

However, the means of combating these Archons is simply to starve them of fear by the act of laying down our arms and coming together in brotherly love.

To achieve this however will take time as we have, in a way, a "chicken and egg" situation. To defeat the Archons we need peace but, to create peace we need to defeat the Archons.

However, we are not alone in this battle. The most important thing is a natural cycle that is occurring that is moving the galactic system into a time of peace.

As the effect of this is felt by more and more people so the tide will turn.

This will happen, it is inevitable and the Archons know this which is why they are putting so much effort into a last-ditch attempt to cause chaos.

It is the nature of Archons that, if they can't have something, they will destroy so that no one can have it.

So we must be on the "Qui Vive" for any, by psychopaths being influenced by Archons, to create a nuclear war.

Once again, we will get help should this idea come to fruition and a nuclear war will not be allowed to happen.

Thus the ultimate destiny of man is to live in peace.

The period that we are all going through at the moment is just the start. This period of peace will grow over time and will, indeed, last for many thousands of years just as the period of negativity lasted for many thousands of years.

We might consider life as an invisible wave of energy rising and falling over vast periods of time.

Fortunately, we have struck the nadir, the most negative part, so the only way is up towards positivity. It all happens slowly.

The speed that it happens is, in part, connected to something called collective consciousness and so, as very few people are actively working for good at the moment, the rise in consciousness is limited but, each day, more and more people wake to up their spiritual origins so, with each person that takes the path towards God, so the ascension accelerates.

Thus the destiny of man is to live in peace with himself and his fellow man.

Further, as mankind awakes to his spiritual reality, so he will discover that he does, indeed, contain these seven auras associated with him and will develop the desire to explore these auras and the dimensions upon which they are placed. This will eventually open the door to the development of a number of accomplishments that would seem almost magical at the moment.

It must be borne in mind that man is made by the God force and is God like should he realise it.

Just as, in the past, beings thought of as angelic came and interacted with certain people and were observed to have what were thought of as angelic gifts, so man is a similar angelic being and would have similar powers.

The people who saw angelic beings, saw them as beings of light.

Now, vibration is closely connected to light.

Further, the most important power in the universe is consciousness.

Thus, if a person had his God consciousness greatly developed, his body, which is under the control of his consciousness would, perforce, change.

As God consciousness is light, the more God consciousness a person incorporates into his personality, the more it will effect change in his physical body. Therefore, if a person was truly imbued with God consciousness, his body would start to glow with God's light, a spiritual light shining in the dark.

This is the destiny of all mankind, to become beings of light living on a planet of light.

There would be no place for darkness.

One day, everything will be aglow with spiritual light.

Does this sound like a fairy tale?

Maybe it does at the moment but the ascension movement is just at its beginning. In time, as man draws into his auras the God force, and as that God force enters his physical body, so that God force, which manifests itself as light, will transform the human body into a body of light reflecting to all the transformative power of God.

Light is actually all that exists, as the only thing that exists is the God force (life) and that God force is the light of God.

Can you imagine being a being of light like an angel?

Possibly not, but it is entirely possible if not probable right now.

However, for future generations it will become fact.

How long this transformation will take depends on each individual and also the collective consciousness.

But it will happen.

Further, other magical effects will occur.

The collective and individual consciousness is closely connected to the God force.

God, the creator of all that is, does not put a limit on itself.

So we will have no limit on ourselves as we advance towards God. The only limit will be the limits that we impose on ourselves.

So, somewhat magical events will be perfectly possible.

Teleportation will be the standard form of transport, as it is in the astral realms.

Telepathy will be the normal form of contact as it is in the higher realms.

Food will be made from the ether. It actually is now but, due to the limitations of the planet's, and our, level of spirituality, it has to pass through physical things.

Further, the spiritual force that imbues all things will manifest itself in creating a more vibrant planet.

Your home planet (Earth), will shake off its blanket of negativity that has for so long cloaked it, the negative thoughts of man's creation, and reveal its true colors.

The color of the sky will be a more vibrant blue and the flowers of the field will grow in such profusion and with such colors that would be unimaginable at the moment.

Naturally, there will be no slaughter of animals as sustenance will be created from the ether.

Animals will become our friends rather than our victims and will be left to prosper as nature intended, nurtured by man rather than exploited.

Thus will all life live in peace and harmony together as one, as was intended.

The change will come slowly but it behoves all who can to speed that day by meditating, praying and by respecting all life.

Thus we wish to make it plain to all that the dark world in which you have all lived for so long is changing. Life is progressing from the negative concept, which is all any of you have known, up into a world of light.

Light chases darkness. Darkness disappears as soon as light is projected into it.

Darkness is an illusion. If it was real, light could not make it disappear but the simple fact that light shone into any area of darkness transforms it into light thus demonstrates that darkness is an illusion.

God's light is starting to illuminate the world and shine into the collective consciousness. Thus it is inevitable that, in the degree that light illuminates every corner of God's creation, darkness will disappear, leaving the evil ones exposed for who they really are.

With God's light comes love, love for all things and, where there is love and light, there cannot be fear.

Fear is created by shutting out light and making people live in the dark.

People are naturally afraid of the dark because they do not know what menace might exist in a corner, lurking, waiting to attack a defenceless person.

However, once we shine light into that area we quickly see that in all probability there was nothing there to fear except fear itself.

It was mentioned earlier that the driving force of Archons is fear. Thus they have, for long ages created darkness - spiritual darkness if not actual darkness - so that people live in fear, which helps energise the Archons.

Light is coming and the day will arrive when the worst fear of the Archons will happen, exposure.

The Archons secret, the key to their success was secrecy. Secrets can only be kept if there is no exposure and so they have tried their best to keep light from shining on them.

They are doomed to fail.

Light is coming and the day will arrive when they will be exposed alongside the people they have victimised, the psychopaths that have both ruled you and kept you in the dark.

When this day occurs, and it will, we must turn to God and become Godlike in our response to them.

We must forgive them - for they know not what they do.

In a way they are innocent because to behave in a psychopathic way is all they know.

Equally, their masters, the Archons, do not know any other behaviour than what they are programmed by time to do, so it would not be correct to punish them even if such a thing were possible.

But, equally, there would be no place either for Archons or psychopaths in this new, light filled world, so a way must be found to isolate them from the rest of humanity.

This will be happening in a spiritual manner anyway.

As most of humanity starts to fill themselves with light and spiritual power, the relatively few psychopaths that, remember, have no access to the light will be left, scratching their heads and wondering just what is going on.

However, they have not been removed from power yet and so we do not need to take a decision as to how we will deal with these evil people.

One thing is certain, their time is over.

Their power is fading.

Light is already shining on them and revealing their negative actions.

Already the Archons, and their minions are feeling this light penetrating their world, revealing their dark secrets.

So we advance in peace drawing the power of God towards us, filling ourselves, slowly, with light, shining that light into the world, illuminating the dark corners, removing darkness, removing fear and replacing it with love.

This is the destiny, the goal of man - to become a being of light, a reflection of the God force.

CHAPTER TWO

THE GREAT DIVIDE

When this creature we call man was created for, make no mistake, everything that exists was created, he was made of spiritual matter, etheric essence, the God force.

Thus, he was not only a spiritual force but he was, in essence, the life force we call God.

Now, one tends to think of God as all intelligent, all knowing, containing infinite wisdom concerning any subject and it is true that, today, we can give those attributes to God. But it was not always so.
By its very nature God, having created all life, did so in order to gain knowledge so, logically, there must have been a time when God was without knowledge.

This, obviously, was a long time ago. A time so distant that it would be almost impossible to imagine it.

But, nevertheless, this life force existed, the only thing that existed in an empty void.

Over eons of time this life force, having curiosity, thought about how to explore, create, manifest its life force into some form of reality and so, as was mentioned in chapter one, it created a number of bands, each one separate from another from another by distinct frequencies that we call carrier waves.

So now, we have in an empty void, the life force that we refer to as God, being a simple, uneducated - for want of a better word - force and eight distinct bands, also empty but awaiting the moment when this life force would start to inhabit these eight bands of frequency.

We wish you to comprehend that, at that moment in time, absolutely nothing existed in any of these dimensions, neither physical, etheric or astral.

Indeed, these terms had no meaning. All that existed was eight bands of vibration and a life force.

This, obviously was before the, so called, "big bang", this imaginary event that science has erroneously invented in a futile attempt to explain how the visible universe came into being.

In fact, there was no explosive moment when planets suddenly appeared as will be made apparent. Science, once again, in observing the physical creation is merely observing the final effect of a process that started in much higher realms.

So, if science hopes, one day, to locate the point of origin of creation they must put down their measuring instruments and begin to work with their spiritual faculties, for the answers to their questions will be found in those areas.

Now, curiosity, the desire to create the means to express itself, pushed this God force to take action. It must be remembered that the God force is also vibration, far above the vibrational field of any of the eight bands that had been created, but it is a vibrational force.

Indeed, if it was not vibrating, it would not have had the idea to create these eight bands also vibrating. It was like-constructing-like.

So we would like you to imagine, if you will, that the God force who, being pure light, was vibrating. As light is a vibrational force, so it created eight versions of itself, each one of a lower, denser frequency until the lowest one shone with very little light. This lowest band is the one in which physical life was ultimately created. However, each one of these bands existed only as potentials, being bereft of any life form.

It occurred to God that, in order to create any forms to inhabit these bands, these carrier waves, it would have to lower its frequency, split itself into eight and put itself into each of these bands.

This, it did.

However, it was not much further forward as God itself did not have any form, so nothing existed in these bands of vibration except the God force itself.
But God, being life, was able, over vast amounts of time, to create one essential life force that had something that could be called intelligent life - a form of man.

Man was God's first creation.

Once again, God was not much further forward. God had created this life force in its highest plane of vibration but this life force was, itself, a sort of copy of God, albeit with a form that we would recognise as man, but this was a pure spiritual force, pure light, but itself with no more experience than God itself.

So God gave this life force - man - the means to think, to explore and to wonder why it existed.

Thus, to help this creation, God manifested space and time in a higher dimensional form than man incarnate could imagine and he furnished this space/time with planets and all that exists on the highest plane to this day.

The object was to provide this human being with experiences that would help him educate himself and thus grow in wisdom.

We should point out at this moment that it is actually a picture that we are painting rather than strict truth because the actual events, the vast amount of time involved and the processes undertaken to create all this would make the actual events incomprehensible to modern man incarnate at the moment - you - the reader, but is, in essence, true and close enough to reality that we feel comfortable presenting this story to you in order to give you a basis for understanding the origins of man.

So, at this point we have these eight carrier waves of vibration (light), but only the highest one containing any form of life and that life was man.

This early man explored the astral world that God had created and fed that information back into the original God force and this force started to grow in wisdom.

It is not known just how many versions of itself in human form God created but there were sufficient, not only to explore this band of frequency - the eighth dimension - but, once God had created them he stopped. So the number of humans that God created at that time is the same number that exists today.

In fact, although we have explained it in this fashion to help you understand, we must admit that what we have said is not the total truth.

We stated, earlier, that all life is one, so God was only able to create what we might imagine to be just one entity. This, as you can imagine, was not what God had in mind because, not only did he create eight different bands of carrier waves but, in order to obtain a maximum amount of experience God found a way of creating a vast number of consciousnesses.

Thus, although there is only one life force (God), nevertheless, there are a huge number of expressions of that consciousness which, in effect, creates the illusion of a huge number of humans of various shapes and forms because, it is not necessary for all humans to have the same exact form as you are accustomed to seeing.

Indeed, even on Earth, there are virtually no two people exactly the same.

There are people with different skin colors, different head shapes, different eyes, noses and mouths. Different heights and body forms.

Therefore, no two people are identical.

The basic human form of having a head, body, two arms, two legs is what is considered to be what makes a human form.

So the various consciousness that God created is what gives each human form its unique identity.

We repeat, in order to make this quite clear that, at some distant point in the past, God created one single entity that could be considered to be a human but he instilled into that human a virtually unlimited number of consciousnesses rather as one might imagine a person with what is called split personalities although, of course, this was not an illness but a deliberate act on the part of God to create as many expressions of itself as were considered necessary to experience life to the full, ultimately.

This will, of course, be difficult for some people to realise that, although they have a distinct, unique body, hidden behind that body, at its base concept it is one with all life, past, present and future.

There is only one life and that life is God.

Now, we must remember that this splitting of itself into multiple consciousnesses was taking place in the eighth dimension.

So we need to visualise that, in that dimension, the highest in terms of vibration that exists, this unique life force was able to manifest itself as an enormous number of different consciousnesses.

This was all well and good but the God force required more from its creation.

There was no point in just having countless points of consciousness, countless points of life floating in a sea of vibration which represented the carrier wave of the eighth dimension.

These points of consciousness were just aspects of life, with no experience, no sense of self, of personality. Not even a sense that it was human.

We break off here to state that, although we have been concentrating on humanity and will continue to do so as the intention of this book is to explain the history of man, the God force also created other versions of itself that would be used to create other life forms.

This book would be impossibly complicated, not to say to become an unwieldy tome if we tried to incorporate the history of every life form in the multiverse, so we need, perforce, to ignore the other life forms and just follow our quest along the path that mankind took.

So, we have an eighth dimension and, within the vibrational field of that dimension, we have the God force representing itself as many forms of consciousness that would, eventually, take the form of mankind.

However, in this eighth dimension, the consciousness created by God could be compared to an embryo child: a potential without actual form of any sort of life dynamic that we could associate with.

Just a life force.

This is where things will start to become even more difficult for some people to appreciate or comprehend.

The desire of God was not to create entities that were copies of itself. Its desire was to create objects that could think for themselves, go forth and have experiences that would enrich the God force and help it grow in wisdom.

This desire to grow in wisdom is the dominant driving force for most people.

So a way of organising a system to enable this to take place was conceived.

It was decided by God to manifest what can best be described as problems. Not problems that beings incarnate would recognise, but challenges to intelligence that would push human consciousnesses, present in that eighth dimension, to investigate and overcome.

These challenges, these problems, would not be considered difficult by modern man except that, occurring in the highest spiritual plane that God had manifested, required these original humans to think in terms of spirituality to overcome them.

Just what these little problems were is of no interest to comprehend because they were resolved so long ago by early man that they no longer concern us and also, to be honest with you, they would not relate to anything with which you are familiar and thus would, in all probability, not be understood by the majority.

So please accept that this early form of man was presented with these problems that pushed him to use his intuition and intelligence, limited as it was, to overcome them.

It is a fact that life evolves through experience. All experience presents itself as a challenge of some sort and compels us to think about the experience being undergone and to incorporate that experience - and its resolving - into its life force.

Thus, slowly, early man developed what can be described as wisdom as a result of resolving these simple problems.

This was the beginning of creating man in a truly recognisable form, not only in a physical, albeit astral sense, but also in a sense of having wisdom to deal with problems.

Man, as we understand it to be could not exist in purely physical form, whatever plane of existence it would find itself on. Man must also contain a mental component, wisdom, knowledge or even cunning before it can truly be called "man".

So this was a giant step forward for the development of man, and God decided to use it as the basis for all his future attempts to push his experiment forward.

Already, by the number of consciousnesses that were presented with identical problems, it was noticed by God that a number of different approaches for solving these problems were undertaken and this pleased God. It was exactly what it was looking for, independent thought about problem solving.

So, still on this highest plane, God created more and more problems for his creation, man, to solve and each time the solutions were fed back into the God force in their entirety and thus the God force itself began to develop wisdom in problem solving, as did the manlike consciousness present in the eighth dimension.

We will not bore you by describing the eons of time this continued, the mountains of problems these early beings were presented with, the steps they took to resolve these problems. Suffice to say that, if we jump forward today to that eighth plane of vibration, every conceivable problem that could ever exist has been experienced and resolved and all that vast amount of information has been fed into the God force.

Thus we can say, today, that God is infinite wisdom and, once a human evolves to the eighth plane, he too will be infinitely wise and at the equivalent level of wisdom as God itself.

That is the reason that the God force reabsorbs that supremely wise and knowledgeable conscious back into itself as it has completed its journey through time and has become one again with the God force that created it in the beginning long, long ages ago.

So, we break off here to suggest to you, the reader, not to try to avoid problems because it is inevitable that they will appear, but to use the God force that is called your higher self to call forth the solution.

One must remember that God made us all as consciousness, reflections of itself and this God force contains both information about any problem conceivable and also the answer.

This God force has been placed in association with you.

Some call it your "soul", although that is not strictly true as the soul is just a protective shell surrounding and protecting the God spirit but, in essence it is the same as spirit and soul travel together until the God spirit merges once more with its creator, God, and at that point, both the God spirit and the shell - soul - disappear.

The point being made is that you, and every person, has this all-knowing God spirit associated with you so the solution to any problem is available if you know how to make contact with your higher self and draw the appropriate response to any problem from its vast stock of solutions.

We repeat, the answer to any problem that could ever come to you, whatever its form, whatever its complexity, is available because it is stored within your personal aspect of God, known as your higher self, thanks to the vast years spent by early, spiritual, man finding solutions to problems presented by the God force and by feeding both the questions and the answers back to God. It is thanks to these courageous, industrious, early versions of man that these solutions are given to you and you should be grateful.

Have you noticed, however, that the vast majority of humanity incarnate today face each problem as if it were occurring for the first time and stumbles through error after error in an attempt to resolve the problems when the answer is sitting and waiting to come forth from their higher self if only contact with that higher self could be made? Researching the solution to that problem will be dealt with in a later chapter as we wish to continue exploring the development of early non-physical man.

Suffice to say that any problem you could be confronted with was created by the God force long ago, so any solution to that problem was already discovered long ago and it is all available to you because you are that God force.

There is never any need to dread problems arriving on your doorsteps. They may be presented to you by another person or event but both the person or event are the God force manifest in man or the situations that man creates, so the solution is also instantly available to you, if and when, you can draw it from the God force, your higher self.

The day people realise this a great change will occur. People will realise that there is no point in trying to create difficulties for others because they are drawing these difficulties from their higher selves and the recipient of those difficulties already has the solution disponible as he draws that solution from his higher self.

When this happy day arrives will be the day that man learns to live in peace together ceasing to create problems for each other but banding together as one to resolve the inevitable problems that life itself creates in its thirst to create more wisdom for itself.

Problems will always occur but worry will cease as someone, somewhere in creation, will be able to draw the solution to that problem and make it available to those seeking the solution.

Thus will God continue in its endless quest for wisdom by creating problems and receiving solutions. It is not the solution that interests God but the steps taken by man to resolve the problem.

Thus does God grow ever wiser and thus will man grow ever wiser.

However, to return to the subject under discussion.

We have man in the eighth carrier wave, dimension, now long years into the future, infinitely wise, having solved every problem that the God force could think to present to it.

But still the other bands of frequency, of lower frequency than the eighth, remain empty.

The next logical step was to find a way of transferring man into those lower dimensions, one step at a time.

So, in order to do this, something else needed to be thought about: how to lower the frequency of at least some of the humans on the eighth plane down into the seventh without disturbing the frequency of the eighth plane and the entities that it contains.

So the first step was to request volunteers, humans that were willing to be moved in frequency down from the eighth dimension to a lower one. This took a certain amount of courage by the humans living in the eighth dimension as it would be a leap in the dark.

However, the God force had created all of these planes identical, as has already been mentioned so, when the volunteers arrived on this seventh plane it seemed familiar.

Now, the process of changing from one frequency, one carrier wave, one dimension to another is, of course, a spiritual one. We are still dealing with spiritual forces.

God, quite simply, took these volunteers, one by one, and enveloped them in a sort of protective shell, rather as an embryo chick is encased in an egg shell and "bombarded" that person with a frequency that corresponded with the vibration of the seventh dimension.

Thus the person disappeared from that eighth dimension and found himself in the seventh.

This continued until all who chose to put themselves forward for transfer were sent to the seventh plane and these humans, now on a world identical to the one that they had left except that, as it was of a lower frequency, the light was less brilliant.

So, having acclimatised to this new plane, natural curiosity pushed them to want to explore this world.

In what we might call a topographical sense the landscape was already known, being identical to the one they had just left but the beings that had arrived realised that God must have created it for some reason and wondered what that reason was.

There would have been no point in God creating an identical situation on the seventh dimension as had been created on the eighth - problem and solution - so God put another plan into action.

This was the concept of creating auras, by which is meant that a living being living on the seventh dimension could also retain a connection to the eighth.

Thus the humans that God created to inhabit the seventh dimension were able to retain a perfect connection to the higher dimension, the eighth plane where, we remember, that solutions to any problems were retained.

However, it was deemed necessary to create new experiences on this seventh plane and thus God put into the minds of these humans the desire to explore, physically, the various planets that God had also created.

It must at all times be remembered that this dimension is what would be termed astral and thus explorations undertaken were of an astral sense.

But it must also be realised that these planes, dimensions, although not physical when regarded from an Earthly perspective seem, nevertheless, real and as solid as the Earthly plane seems to the humans that live on that plane.

So early humanity set out to explore these diverse planets but, to their dismay, there was nothing much to see. No new experiences to be gained.

You will remember that God's driving aim, the reason that it went to all the trouble to create everything was to gain knowledge.

Empty planets provided little or no knowledge.

So God decided to put other life on these planets.

These other life forms were early versions of the animals that are today observed on Earth.

It must be understood that their "physical" appearance, for want of a better word, bore little resemblance to the animals that we see on the surface of the planet Earth. It would be better to say that they were life forms different from human life forms.

These different life forms existed already in the eighth dimension but we have avoided mentioning them much in order to not confuse our examinations of human origins.

However, we are now in a position, on the seventh plane where we must consider early man's interactions with these non-human life forms that we will still call animal.

Compared to man at this point who had access to the solutions to all the problems, thanks to the work accomplished in the eighth plane, these animal forms were totally "primitive", once again for want of a better word.

By primitive, we mean without the benefit of any of the knowledge and wisdom that man had acquired at that point.

Thus these animal life forms were wandering about the seventh plane, no doubt feeling somewhat lost and wondering what life held in store for them.

They observed the presence of man sharing the astral planets of that seventh plane with them but without the means to comprehend who and what these humans where and what, if any, their interaction with these human beings would bring them in terms of experience.

Indeed, just like early man who started up on the eighth plane long years before, they were totally without any means to make any connection with man.

This is where God prodded man to take action to interrelate with these animal life forms.

It became quickly obvious to man that any form of intellectual interchange with these animals would be quite impossible, so early man took another approach and tried sowing the seeds of love and affection. This did work. The animals responded to affection and drew close to man as man tried to investigate just who and what these animal forms were.

So, one step was towards understanding was achieved. The animals could understand love.

Although early man may not have been aware of the reason why love worked, we now know that it was because the animals were created by God and God, being just one life force, was the same life force that created man. Therefore, both man and these animals under investigation were all aspects of the one creator, and so points of consciousness projecting from the one life force. Thus the animals and the humans were one with God.

As God is total light and love, both man and the animals responded to love in an effort to rejoin the God-force that sent them out from itself so long ago.

So, through the bond that love makes these animals came close to man and followed man about as he investigated the astral planets of the seventh plane.

We break off our investigations of early man once again to point out that this bond of love still exists to this day. Man still feels the desire to share his life with animals, that he now calls "pets".

Any and all animals, if brought close to the love projected by man at an early age, accept the love and are keen to bond with man.

Not only cats and dogs. Animals of all descriptions will accept the love of man.

Thus we see animals of the widest variety link with man and we see humans caring for insects, mammals of all descriptions from mice to the huge felines and elephants, fish and every conceivable creation of the animal kingdom. They all respond to the love and care man gives animals and these animals respond within the limits of their abilities to so respond.

It is the link of love that causes this and this love comes from the deep realisation that all life is one.

To return to the seventh plane. We mentioned that animals followed man around as he explored the astral planets.

Thus animals began to investigate the parts of these planets that did not, necessarily, attract the attention of early man.

The animals explored caves and grottoes. They climbed high mountains and underground areas. They took to water, albeit in an astral sense.

Gradually, once again over eons of time, a more recognisable form of animal came into being.

Some, indeed many, broke away from the love and care of man and took up independent identities in the fields, forests, seas, lakes, caves and mountain tops.

Gradually they lost interest in man and man in them and they started to create their own experiences.

This, once again, was what God desired. All the experiences acquired by these early animals was fed into the God force and so God grew in wisdom thanks to the animal's experiences.

This complex interplay between man and beast played out for a long time as early man tried to fine tune his relationship with the animal kingdom.

Some animals, over time, became distinctly wary of man and, equally, man became wary of the now wild animals.

Many animals remained close to man and a symbiosis between man and these friendly animals became strong and love bonds were formed.

However, the other creatures distanced themselves from man and, indeed, distanced themselves from other species unlike them until distinct groups were formed, each group forming specific packs of species, each one only feeling "at home" with fellow creatures of their own group or pack.

Fortunately, at that time, the concept of killing and the need for eating was not part of that reality and so the various groups of animals contented themselves with living apart from each other.

It must also be said that the concepts of fear and hatred were also unknown either to man or beast at that stage, so the various groups lived in relative peace and when one group of animals crossed the path of another group, they passed each other and continued on their way in peace.

Man also played a role in this theatre.

His job, at that time, as directed by the God instinct that he contained, was to try to act as an intermediary force between the various groups of animals and seek to bring them back together as friends - for want of a better word - as they were long before.

Needles to say, man's efforts were in vain.

It was too late for man to undo the efforts of long years of separation and so the tribes of animals remain apart to this day.

As early man observed the behaviour of these disparate groups of animals, the concept, the idea that it might be a good idea if they, too, separated into disparate groups was born in the minds of early man.

So, once again over vast eons of time, man formed small "families" of people of similar mindset to themselves, and started to live apart from others.

Then, by the never ceasing law of mutual attraction - like attracting like - other likeminded people joined a group and the groups grew and expanded over time.

Eventually a more (to us) recognisable form of world came into being. A world where groups of animals lived apart from each others group and groups of man of similar outlook to each other started to band together into clans, villages and tribes not dissimilar to what is observed among primitive groups of people on Earth to this day.

The concept of tribalism was formed amongst man.

The concept of separatism was formed in animals.

These concepts were the birth of the very same effects that continue throughout the dimensions to this day, for do not think that discarnate man lives in universal brotherhood. Far from it.

Although man in his body of light cannot kill he can feel separateness from others should he wish and many do.

Equally, wild animals, when discarnate, still tend to live in packs in their universe and do not lose the sense of separateness.

We look forward to the day when man and beast, both incarnate and discarnate can live together in peace and love but the idea of separateness created so long ago is deeply ingrained and it will take a long time before this primitive concept will fade and be replaced with man and beast roaming the plains and rocky areas in peace together as was intended originally.

CHAPTER THREE

THE ILLUMINATION OF MAN

In the beginning, long before anything that we would recognise as life existed there was, nevertheless, a life force.

This life force we have already mentioned and we called it God. This life force - God - has always existed as far as is known.

It would be logical to question where this God-force came from for nothing can appear out of the blue by magic.

But there are a few things about which even the wisest amongst us has no knowledge. We have to have an open mind about things, use our intelligence to puzzle out what seems logical and what seems ridiculous.

It is obvious that something that we call life exists and so it must be obvious that something must have created that life.

We accept that the originator of life is this mysterious, unfathomable force we term God. As has been mentioned previously, where God came from is not known by anyone.

We understand the desire that many have had, stretching back for long ages, to resolve this mystery but no one has yet found the answer.

The origin of God is unknown.

What is known is that this force we call God has always existed and is responsible for the creation of all life in all dimensions and throughout all time.

It is further known that this force we call God has created all that exists as a spiritual force, because of the need to manipulate everything according to the desire of God to create experience.

Thus it became apparent that whatever this force we call God is, one thing is certain.

It is a force of infinite power.

Among these powers is the ability to create illusion. This, if anyone has followed the various teachings already transmitted to you, must be obvious by now.

So great is this illusionary force that, to try to explain how life is constructed, we have, ourselves, time and again, been obliged to use subterfuge to explain the points we have been trying to illustrate.

This does not please us and is not our goal, but the reality of the construction of all life is complex and to launch ourselves into a factual explanation of reality - as far as it exists - would have been pointless.

We apologize for confusing you with tales, with what might be considered stories related to young children by parents trying to explain sophisticated elements taken from life.

This concept of story telling instead of relating truth has been used by many great teachers over the years. The master Jesus often used parables to illustrate spiritual points he wanted to make and other teachers often used childish descriptions when trying to explain their understanding of who God was for instance.

There are many people today that would have difficulty in accepting God as an abstract force, completely devoid of any desire to influence life but, in opposition, just desirous of absorbing the knowledge that the experiences of his creations offered.

Thus, often, God is presented as a person controlling the world, offering blessings, granting wishes and pardoning or condemning people in an arbitrary fashion.

This is, of course, quite understandable when we look at past people whose level of education and whose ability to think clearly was limited.

It is, perhaps, relevant to our discussion of life to question why man, just a few centuries ago had such a limited ability to analyse life and thus to understand more clearly the nature of God.

People talk about evolution.

Usually, when evolution is discussed reference is made to physical aspects of the subject under discussion - how, in the case of man, for example, body shape has altered as food has become more plentiful for most, hygiene and eating habits have improved and so on - but reference is seldom made to the evolution of the spiritual part of man.

And yet, one would have thought that examining and analysing the changes in spiritual attitudes would have been of considerable importance in quantifying who man is, what he has become in comparison to what he was a relatively short time in the past.

Much time is, and has been, spent comparing earlier man to modern man, not only in physical form but also in mental abilities, in the construction of so called "civilisation"; housing, transport and providing comfort, but who has ever stopped to examine and compare the spiritual qualities of earlier man compared to today?

Has anybody ever compared the spiritual growth of man over the years?

It might be postulated that the opposite is the case. It might be thought probable that man's spiritual progression has been at a standstill for long ages.

One could suggest that, as witches are no longer burned at the stake and that heretics are no longer punished or killed that some progress has been made.

However, even that is not true.

At the moment when this book is being produced, in a number of countries it is common practice that people committing the "sin" of unauthorised dress-wear or of eating the wrong food, consuming the wrong beverages are punished in a horrific fashion or beheaded in public for the delight of the spectators.

Now, as all life is one, until such barbaric practices stop, none of us can say we have progressed spiritually at all.

This criticism applies also to us who live in the higher frequencies.

All life is one and so all life is at the same spiritual level. There cannot actually be some people more advanced spiritually than others if we are all one.

Until the least advanced spiritually among us rejects hateful thoughts and turns to love, none can rest in the halls of peace and tranquility.

If one considers the human population as a whole, what real progress, spiritually, has been made?

Which religions have revised their teachings in recent times to incorporate the spiritual knowledge available?

No, it must be admitted that, for the vast percentage of the world's population, little or no improvement has occurred.

The reason for this was discussed in chapter one.

We mentioned the stranglehold that the Archons have maintained on humanity for many long years so that they may profit in negative energy creation by the various processes they have installed in order to keep mankind in a state of discord and conflict.

But we also mentioned that change, positive change, was and is coming to Earth in all the dimensions, physical and astral, which will open the door to a more harmonious form of living.

This, of course, will take a certain time but success is assured. The speed that change will occur is, as has been mentioned, dependent on the speed that all mankind can accept the influx of this positive energy flooding into man and can release his negative aspects.

But, as is always the case, to assist in keeping things in balance, there must be an increase in negative vibration.

It may be difficult to appreciate but, if there was a sudden, monumental influx of positive energy flooding into humanity, chasing out all negativity in an instant, this might be considered to be a wonderful thing but the reality would be chaos.

Too much of a good thing.

All changes must happen slowly. Good gently prising bad out, a step at a time.

So the Archons, who are doing all that they can to maintain the status quo in an evil sense are actually playing into the hands of the angelic beings introducing positivity but using Archon influence as a hand brake to help counter balance positivity to avoid chaos from happening.

One wonders what the Archons, who are the epitome of evil, would think if they were able to realize that the positive angelic beings are using them to assist in the gentle inflow of pure love.

Fortunately, the Archons, being so enwrapped in evil are not able to see outside of their negative control system and thus could not comprehend to what use they are being put.

The same applies, of course, to the psychopaths currently in incarnation. They, too, are being used to slow the influx of positivity to avoid chaos, but they, also, are so involved in negativity that they cannot see that they are being made use of.

As this inflow of positivity is being introduced slowly in order to give humanity a chance to develop slowly and gradually, so the negative forces are of the opinion that they are winning the battle between good and bad, love and evil and are celebrating what they see as a certain and close victory.

They will, ultimately, be deceived, of course. But, by the time that they realize the game that has been played on them by the positive forces, it will be too late. The battle will be over.

However, we ask you to be patient and courageous.

Victory is assured but each move on the universal chess board takes time as each move must hide the master plan for victory by allowing the enemy to think that he is winning.

Check mate is assured but the pawns and various other pieces must be played and moved into position carefully.

There is no room for error.

As this great game is being played on many levels of reality, it must be realized that the overall picture of life is constantly moving. Just as with most things, there is the ebb and flow of events rising and falling as the way life is viewed. Sometimes we have the image that peace is winning and sometimes we think that evil has the upper hand.

The truth is that, for many millennia, evil did have priority and it seemed perfectly normal that wars, hatred, bloodshed and evil were the natural way for life to evolve, both human and animal but, following the great procession of life, change always occurs.

Evil cannot reign forever. Neither can peace and love but, fortunately, we have moved from the downward flow. As all things must ultimately balance we must now start to move into the upward swing so we move into a period which also will last for many millennia.

In order for this new way of living to become reality, enormous changes must take place in all the dimensions, physical and astral.

As was mentioned, these changes must take place slowly so that all life can adapt to the changes.

We should now consider how these changes will affect man dressed in his physical body and his bodies of light. We must also consider man's home, when incarnate - planet Earth - and study the life forms that live on the planet and how these changes will affect them.

Man has been under the influence of the negative forces for so long that history has based its investigations solely on these dark periods.

The last time there was a bright, positive time was so long ago that recorded history has no recollection of that time.

Fortunately, in the spiritual realms, there are people whose memories go back that far and we can record their recollections in order for us to map out and predict how the move into the light might occur.

So we, who have planned this book, have contacted these wise beings and have asked their help in recounting how life evolved at that time.

As all life moves in similar cycles, it is expected that their memories will be able to act as a blueprint for us to be able to predict for you what will happen.

It should be noted that:
(a) we are in the early stages of this upward swing and,
(b) we will be describing what will occur over many, many, millennia so the people who will be able to read this book will have moved on to other pastures long before it all will come to fruition.

However, it is expected that, eventually, man discarnate will be able to communicate with future man incarnate and will be able to pass the information down to him to help guide his passage through his incarnation.

It should be realised that this book, which is being dictated from spirit and which, it is hoped will be published on Earth eventually, is a copy of a book, the original, which will be kept for all time in the libraries of the spiritual planes.

So this information will never be lost and will, it is hoped and expected, be made available in printed or electronic form on Earth for man incarnate to read but also be available for man dressed in his bodies of light to read.

So let us look at some of the ways that life should start to change.

We must first consider the reasons why it was necessary for humanity to develop its level of spirituality above and beyond the level of knowing that a force called God existed and the concept of heaven and hell put into place in the hopes of curbing the wildest excesses of zeal both in a religious and demonic sense, the one sometimes not being far from the other.

Once humanity had developed beyond the point of what we would call caveman and had developed sufficient intellect so as to be able to quantify for himself the more mysterious aspects of life, it became clear that a control system was required.

Thus, as was mentioned, our arch enemies, the Archons, made their appearance on the stage of life, first in an astral sense and later, working through the minions that they had co-opted to their will, in a more physical, practical fashion.

The Archons and Archon controlled people introduced the concepts that we call religions, complete with teachings both based on fact and based on falsehood. Either way, a very selective version of spirituality was presented to the world, virtually ignoring any mention of love, peace and happiness and concentrating on hell and damnation for any person who dared to step outside of the strict parameters set by the Archons for conducting their lives.

These concepts, although first introduced into the minds of man many thousands of years ago are still alive today.

So, although man progressed, slowly, in a technological sense over the centuries, from a spiritual aspect virtually no change occurred.

All this was explained at some length in a previous chapter. We merely introduce it again to remind you, briefly, of the history of man, religion and spirituality.

However, as was also mentioned, those unhappy days are now drawing to a close and it is time for the willing to accept what we tell you, to start to enter the next, more glorious phase of existence.

This phase has been awaited in the heavenly spheres for long ages. We knew it was coming and preparations have, for a long time been completed.

Attempts were made from time to time to test the waters by having advanced beings incarnate and give their spiritual message to plumb the depths and observe reactions to these messengers.

At least one being was sent, corresponding to the attitudes of each individual racial group and presenting the same information but from the point of view of each individual race type.

There would have been no point, for example, in a person (a saint) incarnating and presenting information from, say a Christ like perspective to a people whose mindset was totally at variance with the ability to accept such information.

Thus, for one group, Jesus came along and taught his message, Buddha did the same. Krishna and countless others came and taught essentially the same message but presented in a fashion that, it was hoped, would appeal to particular groups of people.

As is so well realized now, much of the teachings fell on stony ground but, nevertheless, these teachings were not wasted.

Although, by and large, either ignored by the general population or corrupted to further fuel the fires of hate and discord, these messages were given and remain as a tribute to the great masters who incarnated in order to help his fellow man.

But the time that the advice of the masters is relevant is over.

We are moving to a new phase in the spiritual development of man.

At the time that the saints incarnated, they were obliged, generally, to teach on an individual basis, converting one person at a time to walk the spiritual path.

Now, from this day forth, vast numbers will feel the inflow of spiritual power and will awaken to the spiritual call. But the strange thing is that people must awaken as individuals.

We use the word "strange" because it flies in the face of logic and in the face of information that we have already given.

If vast numbers are receiving the wakeup call, it would be logical for them all to awaken at the same moment.

Equally, if we are all one, it follows that, if one awakens, all must awaken. But we have just stated that people must awaken as individuals. Clearly, we must explain this contradiction or risk losing all credibility.

To explain, simply, how we can all be one but can act as individuals, we need to return to the concept of consciousness.

Mention was made, both in this book and in other talks given, that God installed in all of us, not only humans but all things, a sense of individual awareness - the desire to grasp hold of the God-force and keep it for himself.

We use consciousness in order to do this. We mentioned that God has self awareness (consciousness) and God installed that self awareness in all things.

Therefore, although all is one and that one is the God-force, the fact is that each element of the total oneness has a sense of self awareness.

Thus it is possible for all to be one but, at the same time, each aspect of that oneness is able to consider itself as a separate element of that oneness.

This is a difficult concept to grasp: all is one but each part of that oneness can act and think separately from all other things.

It is individual consciousness that permits this.

It is an important concept to grasp, that we are one but individual at the same time.

This is part of the extraordinary power of God. To be one and many at the same time.

Consciousness permits this.

So we now have a spiritual force flooding the galaxy, indeed all the dimensions as well, but each and every entity, whatever form it takes; human, animal, plant or mineral must react to that inflowing spiritual force according to how its consciousness accepts and analyses this force.

Some people find it easier to accept the inflowing spiritual force than others. Equally, some animals can do that.

The vegetable and mineral kingdoms are more difficult for us to quantify so we will ignore them in this discussion. Our main focus being man, let us concentrate on how man reacts to this spiritual force.

So, if we ignore all the variations between the two extremes of total acceptance and total rejection, we have these two opposite polarities.

Those who can accept the positive force now pouring into man are helped in this endeavour through the law of mutual attraction in so doing by angelic beings.

At the opposite end of the spectrum, those who cannot accept are aided, through the law of mutual attraction, by the Archons.

Now, as the number of people accepting the inflow of spiritual power increases, so the power of the spiritual force will also increase. Conversely, the power of negativity will decrease in proportion to the power of positivity.

It should be understood by those interested in this subject - the origins of man - that spirituality does not increase in a purely simple mathematical manner. In fact it does not conform to mathematics at all. However, in an effort to enable the student to comprehend, we could say that spirituality increases or decreases exponentially. Thus, for those who can understand that term, the power of God increases or decreases dramatically and the more that people are influenced by this power, it increases or decreases in a manner that quickly becomes more than just the number of people practicing spirituality.

To make the point quite clear, there is little correlation between the power of God flowing into the planet Earth, and its auras, and the actual number of people following spirituality. The power increases dramatically as the number of people increases.

By the same process, the power of negativity decreases dramatically.

However, as was mentioned before, the angelic beings charged with allowing this positive force into man must do it in a controlled fashion as the balance of all things must, at all times, be maintained.

Should these angels lose control of this process, the effect would be catastrophic beyond comprehension.

Thus to the frustration of all good people, those incarnate and those discarnate, patience is required and we must content ourselves with seeing positivity changing the world bit by bit.

Nothing would give us greater pleasure than to see the floodgates open and the world rise to the heights of spirituality that we know is its destiny but, unfortunately, we know the opposite would obtain.

A too rapid unleashing of spiritual power would have the opposite effect and would not achieve the goals anticipated at all.

So what can we expect to happen in the immediate future?

We know that, at the moment, there seems to be a large amount of negativity and we also know that we need to keep some of that negativity in order to maintain balance between positive and negative.

But our goal is to provide conditions in which people find an atmosphere conducive to encouraging them to develop their level of spirituality.

Therefore we put our trust in the angels controlling the balance between good and evil and push forward the spiritual aspects of life knowing that greater minds than ours will control the game.

So we can expect two things to happen. We know that there are an increasing number of people feeling the inflow of this spiritual force and are either turning to prayer, meditation and helping all life or are, at least questioning the old values by which they lived and, through the results of their searching, will start to follow the spiritual path.

Thus will the spiritual power both on the surface of planet Earth and also in its auras increase.

But we must also expect that the number of people doing negative work will seem to increase.

In fact there is no need for more negativity to happen. There are sufficient evil people on Earth at the moment to balance any amount of good, so it will be disclosure of the evil ones that will cause many good people to doubt and thus will lower their level of spirituality and, therefore, keep good and evil in equilibrium.

However, as positivity is a greater force than negativity and, as it is inevitable that this flow of positive power will come to man in increasing volume, so negativity will fade.

These positive forces will generate great changes on man, animal and on the structure of the planet Earth herself eventually.

This, as has been mentioned, will take time but we feel obligated to mention these effects so that the change that will appear over time will not come as a shock to future man. Further, it is hoped that man incarnate at the moment becomes aware of the possible changes so, by dwelling on them he will begin to draw them into his reality.

So let us describe these advances, these changes to all life, as positive spirituality causing alchemical events to occur.

We must bear in mind that God is light. Therefore, as the power of God flows into man, so man will tend to become, eventually, a being of light.

Light can take many forms from the barely visible glimmer of a candle to the blazing brightness of the noonday sun.

Further, light, being life, has its eight auras, as do all things, so these lights in all their various powers will be shining in the astral realms. Indeed, it is in the astral planes that the spiritual light will increase first, to be passed down through the astral dimensions until it finally illuminates the dark plane - planet Earth.

We will just mention that there are also two planes or dimensions beneath Earth that we might term the first and second dimensions but, as neither human nor animal life incarnates in those planes we will ignore them from the point of view of discussing the evolution of humanity and leave them to explore their dark realms alone.

So, gradually, the majority of humanity incarnate and many discarnate will begin to fill their auras with spiritual light.

This will be barely noticeable at first. As was mentioned above, light must come slowly and gradually to avoid trauma, both physical and mental, so the light will fill the planet Earth, and all life, particularly mankind, starting with his auras and working down to his physical body.

This will cause strange sensations in many.

We will have a situation, indeed it has already started, where there will be, despite all the precautions taken, an imbalance of light throughout the various bodies of man. The higher auras will be capable of absorbing a more powerful ray of light than the physical body at any moment of time. Thus the higher elements of many will become out of alignment compared to the lower elements.

This will affect the emotional component of some people as the higher auras respond to the influx of bright light while the lower elements, including the physical part, is still processing a less bright ray.

So it is suggested that people learn to keep a close watch on their emotional attitudes and, if it is suspected that things are going awry, that a halt is made to any spiritual progress until the whole man (physical element and his auras) are capable of absorbing the same light-force.

Only then should anyone continue to try to advance towards God.

God needs strong, well and healthy people to serve him, not an army of mental cripples.

Assuming that due warning is taken, as man meditates and opens himself to light being projected to him, so he will gradually fill himself with this positive energy.

Man, generally, has been for long ages an ego based creature.

This has been the result of the negative forces that have dominated all life, both in the physical domain and in the lower astral dimensions.

It has been a force engineered in order to create the world that surrounds you.

Those people who have ego the most developed are the ones who rise to the top of the pile in terms of finance, political and industrial power.

As these egocentric people control much of the world, by the law of mutual attraction, they draw towards them like minded people and reward these people who are similar to themselves, promoting them to high offices and rewarding them financially.

The ultimate in egocentricity manifests itself in what we term psychopaths, people totally concentrated on their own needs, wants and ambitions.

It will be difficult for light to enter and to have much effect on true psychopaths but it will be able to enter the hearts of many of those employed by psychopaths.

As spiritual light enters the hearts of these people, so they will start to question the aims and motives of their leaders - the true psychopaths.

This will, in some ways, be an effect similar to what was described earlier, people whose physical bodies were at one level of spiritual development while their higher auras were at a more advanced state of development.

In the case of those employed by psychopaths they will start to notice that what they are required to do in their day to day work will be at odds with what they feel comfortable doing.

This will cause much turmoil in the minds of many.

The action taken to resolve this dilemma will depend on the person.

Some will stifle their new, higher emotions and carry on doing the bidding of their masters.

Others will abandon ship and turn to less demanding employment.

Yet others will seek to sabotage the plans of their employers in various ways.

Gradually, over a number of years however, these psychopathic leaders will find themselves isolated and more and more alone as, one by one, those in their employ leave like rats deserting a sinking ship.

No one can run an empire alone.

Therefore, it is expected that these psychopathic leaders of virtually every domain that exists will be forced to abandon as they find themselves the last and only one trying to maintain a hold on something that they can no longer control.

It will be in this fashion that the psychopathic leaders will be forced to resign. They will find, quite simply, that no one would want to work with them and so they will be replaced by new leaders that people will want to work with.

Once again it is the law of mutual attraction that will draw the new leaders of those affected by light.

So the old, evil, dark ways of living will be replaced by everyone working together in a light filled world.

As it is hoped you can imagine, this will all take time. Do not expect to see instant change but it will occur.

CHAPTER FOUR

THE WAY TOWARDS FREEDOM

We have talked at some length about how humanity and, indeed, the whole of life in this galaxy was for a long time under the control of a group of negative entities that are known of as Archons and how they successfully created a negative force that all were obliged to conform to.

We also mentioned that change is the only constant and so this endless pendulum that swings back and forth is now propelling us into a period of positivity.

This period of positivity will last as long as the period of negativity lasted, before the pendulum starts, once again, to swing again towards negativity.

This is the way life functions, swinging endlessly back and forth between spiritual growth and decline.

This swinging motion has been described as the breathing of God, drawing breath in and then expelling it again. This, obviously, is an analogy, using parts of life that people can understand in order to explain a somewhat difficult concept, the flow of life, spiritual life, rising and falling creating a movement towards perfection and moving eventually, back towards chaos.

We could, perhaps, consider why this should happen.

If all life is on a path towards perfection it would seem to be more logical just to move in a straight line from total ignorance about God, to being at one with God itself.

However, life does not work like that.

If one examines the way life often operates on Earth, one observes in virtually all things that objects, what we might describe as living objects; plants, animals of all descriptions and humans start off, from in a non-physical sense, as fairly unsophisticated, grow to maximum maturity and then decline back to the point, more or less, to where they started.

It is this pendulum motion, this swing back and forth from infancy, in a mental sense, to maximum maturity, and then back towards infancy again, sometimes referred to as second childhood.

Once again we observe this effect and have no knowledge as to why this should occur.

It would be interesting to study this phenomenon and try to find out why it happens for, if it occurs with all life and over what is referred to as time - countless millennia - there must be a reason.

The answer will be found in the concept of renewal of energy. Energy must be used to create anything and, if all life, in all its different elements of construction were to travel in an endless straight line from creation to perfection, pretty soon, the energy used to create everything would be consumed and life would run out of energy.

Thus, we require this swing between birth, to maturity, which consumes energy, to decline in which the energy used is returned from whence it came to provide the life force for the next generation of creation.

In the case of 'living' things (for every thing is alive) we can readily observe its effect in the birth, growth, decline and death of a creature or person.

However, in vast amounts of time it is rather more difficult to see.

We can scarcely imagine hundreds of thousands of years and we can certainly not actually observe the passage of such vast amount of time.

Nevertheless, the passage of time follows this same course, and, at one point in time growth energy is used, then the pendulum of time starts to swing back again and that energy is returned to its source, rather like discharging and charging a battery.

So let us try to predict which action uses energy and which action replaces energy when dealing with time and the actions of all life during any one of those two periods.

To save you any doubts concerning these events we will say that any negative action releases energy and any positive action uses and consumes energy.

Thus for the last pendulum swing period, life was going through a negative time and energy was returned to its source, and from now onwards, for an equally long period of time, energy will pour into the galaxy reinvigorating all life.

The batteries, if we are to use this term, are fully charged thanks to the negative intentions of the Archons and their deluded minions and huge amounts of this energy are poised awaiting the turning of the switch that will release this energy.

However, to continue with this electrical analogy, the energy must be released slowly, in a controlled fashion, or its supreme and overwhelming power would cause a fuse to blow.

We apologise for using this simple electrical analogy to describe events taking place but if it allows you to understand the concept of using and replacing energy, it will have served its purpose.

So we are firmly on course for positive energy to be received.

Its effects will be scarcely be noticeable at first but, as the switch is opened more, over time, and more of this spiritual energy is released, so the effects will become more visible.

We, indeed live in blessed times.

It is thanks to all the suffering by so many people and animals for so long that were actually returning energy to the God source, through actions created by the Archonic forces, that we can now benefit from that suffering as we move into the light.

We must be grateful to our ancestors who gave so much so that we can reap the harvest of their labor.

As time does not really exist and all is now, if we are able to realize that difficult to understand concept, we can quite literally link with those people who went through those difficult times and, if we reach out mentally, we can share the lives that those people lived. We can partake in the suffering, both mental and physical, that was imposed on them.

Depending on the age we return to and the country we select to observe we can visualize events of a brutality and cruelty that would be scarcely imaginable in this day and age.

This degree of suffering was brought about also because of the position of the galaxy in regard to what is termed by some as the 'Central Sun', which is not actually a correct appellation. There is no Central Sun, but what there is, is a positioning of the galaxy in or out of alignment of a dynamic spiritual force that does, indeed, shine throughout creation either illuminating the astral realms or leaving them in shadow depending on the relative position of our galaxy with regard to this light.

Until recently, we were moving through the shadow part of this created light.

Indeed, as this light is the spiritual light of the God-force, lack of this light illuminating the souls of man, lead to what we might term the night of life, a time when positive spirituality was almost absent.

Thus, as the mind of man as always active and desirous of researching movement and progress, if man is not influenced by a positive light from God, it nevertheless searches for things to do and invent and, with the aid of the Archons, terrible things were created to satisfy the desire to bring progress into reality.

It must be appreciated that when life was passing through the nadir, the point that was directly opposite the maximum brightness that will eventually be experienced, man was, from a spiritual point of view, in stygian darkness and so negative thoughts were first and foremost in the minds of man and so terrible things came into being - the creations of man cut off from any spirituality.

These acts, that would be hard for us to imagine and certainly would not be accepted today, were considered normal and so many suffered terribly.

However, life was short at that time and so the suffering was equally short lived.

We must appreciate that the actions taken by what we would today consider to be evil people were not considered so.

The opposite of holy is evil, but if people are living in a world of spiritual darkness, they can only receive negative thoughts and therefore take negative actions.

There was no other choice at that time.

As has been mentioned, change is the only constant so, slowly, the galaxy, in a spiritual sense moved back into the light.

Thus there are two factions, two reactions that the change from darkness to light engenders.

The Archons, and those that have actively worked for them, are distinctly shocked by this change. Being negative in orientation and, having been in control of the planet for so long, they could not conceive of any change occurring. Further, because they dwell exclusively in the lower astral forms of life, they have no concept of the overall picture. They do not have any knowledge of the way the great pendulum of life swings back and forth over vast periods of time, and so the world in which they live they thought was the only one possible.

It must also be said that no angelic being bothers to interact with Archons because they know that this group of entities have no concept of holiness and, as a result of cutting themselves off from the light, living in a dark world, they, in all probability, would not be able to perceive shining angelic beings and certainly would not understand what they are and from what dimension they come.

Thus, as the move towards the light becomes more obvious, the effect on the Archons is confusion and fear.

Archons like to create fear in others but, for the first time, they are creating fear in themselves - a strange sensation for them; the biter bit.

As was mentioned earlier, their destiny ultimately, is to be isolated in their dark world as the light from God illuminates all corners of the world, astral as well as physical, and these creatures retreat further and further from the light in an attempt to find a small, dark corner in which to cower.

Despite all the harm for which they have been responsible, it is not our intention to harm the Archons. They, unfortunately, were a necessary part of the cycle of life.

As was mentioned, life used their negativity to return spiritual energy back to the God-head and it is thanks to their negativity that the positive forces can come into action.

So, we do not see the Archons as an enemy. They were a necessary part of the pendulum swing of life but we have no further need for them. Their time is over. Now is the time for Godliness and light.

We mentioned that there were two reactions to the influx of light.
One was the Archon reaction; fear and cowering in a corner and the other is those beings that look forward to bathing in the light from God.

We include in this group not only those who already have an elevated consciousness, but also what we might term 'common or garden' types of people. Those who have no particular propensity for spirituality nor for causing harm. This group we suggest, would be the major part of the population of Earth, ordinary people.

This group also, will feel great confusion as the light from God illuminates their auras and great changes to their emotions will occur.

This group who, for so long, had been under Archon control, will feel the emotion of release from this control and, for the first time in many millennia, will start to feel joy.

Joy is a word that has almost no meaning among the population of Earth.

Whatever form of happiness experienced on Earth, there is always an element of fear remaining in the background.

So ingrained is this element of constant fear that it would, at the moment, be almost impossible for the average person to release it and live in a state of pure joy, pure bliss.

Indeed, it is not quite time yet to release all fear. Fear is part of the fight/flight protection that keeps people safe from invasion by the negative forces circulating in the etheric realms.

Eventually, as has been said, these forces will be swept away by the light of God penetrating every corner of God's empire and flooding every aspect of life in all the dimensions with spiritual light.

Now, the question is, what action can we, who are more aware of spiritual progress, take to help the average person and guide them in realizing that these changes are not only inevitable but positive and so nothing to fear but, indeed, something to welcome?

Unfortunately, we have no right to impose ourselves on others.

Therefore we must wait patiently until they come to us, having noticed a difference between them and us, and having the desire to become more like us.

Then, and only then, we can take them under our wing and explain what is going on and guide them along the path to this new-found freedom - freedom from fear.

We look forward to the day when all the people of the planet are filled with joy all the time.

That day is coming and is closer than you think.

The time for misery and despair is over, but it is only so in the degree that people can free themselves from the old, ingrained, notion that evil is always lurking, ready to pounce on anyone unfortunate enough to lower their guard for a moment.

Whilst it is true that the time of complete freedom from evil is not yet come, nevertheless, there is no need to be fearful.

Evil acts and evil thoughts are being swept away by this spiritual light that is flooding the astral, etheric and physical dimensions.

As has been mentioned one can compare light and darkness, both spiritual like physical.

There is a similar effect.

All light, even the smallest glimmer will chase darkness and reveal it for what it was, pure illusion.

Darkness can only exist in the absence of light and, as light is everywhere now, albeit it not yet at full strength, it is pushing darkness away.

So, we have a choice. Either to live in the light or to accept that to live in the shadows is more familiar and feels safer and so to continue to live in shadow.

Only a fool, when given the option of freedom by living in light compared to slavery by being entrapped in darkness, but it takes a certain courage to step from the relative safety of darkness and being revealed in the light.

Many have taken advantage of darkness by presenting themselves as one thing whilst being another.

Many have prospered by fooling those who also lived in shadow of a false identity.

Politicians, bankers, business people and many church leaders have lived like this for long ages, pretending to be kind, considerate and benevolent people whilst, in reality, they were egocentric beings solely concentrating on promoting their own interests.

This attitude can only work in darkness.

This darkness, being of a spiritual nature is capable of manipulation. It is only when people are living in spiritual darkness can lies and deceptions be perpetrated on gullible people.

Thus many are reluctant to step into the light, both perpetrators and victims.

Once the step into spiritual light is taken, everything changes.

Lies and deception are seen for what they are. There is no place for hidden agendas, hidden programs or hidden motives.

Honesty is seen for what it is and falsehood immediately unmasked.

This, of course, applies to all people. We might be glad if any business man or religious leader who told us a falsehood was unmasked but how many of us could stand in the same light and be revealed also.

How many of us could accept that we could never again tell a falsehood, express an opinion that was not totally honest or have a thought about profiting from someone?

For this is what standing in the light means. Our souls, our deepest thoughts, our darkest secrets, those that we would prefer to take to the grave with us, would be revealed to all.

It must be said that once a person's incarnation is terminated and the person moves on to what is called heaven, his soul will be naked for all to see anyway but it is easier to accept that event happening in what is hoped will be a distant future on a different plane of existence than it occurring now, at this moment.

But to stand in God's light means exactly that.

It was mentioned that lies and treachery can only exist when hidden by darkness. To stand in spiritual light automatically reveals our life both positive and negative.

When this occurs in the heavenly spheres we term it the life review - one's whole life exposed to one and all.

This is exactly what will happen here on Earth when one truly steps into the light.

In effect it is stripping back to its foundation the life lived by someone and then starting again, making a fresh start.

That, of course, was the purpose of confession used in some religions but, as is so often the case, it was corrupted and made non-effective.

It must be said that, years ago, for those living in shadow, with no light to step into, it was rather pointless.

Today however, it is - or will be soon - possible. Eventually, as years pass and more and more light comes to us it will be inevitable.

The way this will happen is as follows; man, indeed all sentient life, is complex and multi-layered, multi-dimensional. People living in physical life consider that the only means of communication is by physical means. We speak, using our voice or by writing. Thus, our thoughts are expressed through physical means, or rather the thoughts that we wish to communicate are expressed by those means. This enables, if we so desire, to have a hidden layer of thoughts that we either keep to ourselves or express solely to the few that we choose to be partners in crime.

However, there is a means of communication that is called telepathy which, essentially, is enabled by two, or more, people reaching out with their auras and passing thoughts through them. The thought passes from one mind, into an aura, is picked up by the other aura of another person and that information passes into the mind of the recipient.

That is the most basic form of nonverbal communication and is, in fact, very close to what is used by speech.

In the case of speech, sound waves are used from the voice box of one person into the ear of a second but sound is just vibration.
In the case of telepathy, it is also vibration that is used but more closely resembles wireless telephones that exist today.

However, when dealing with auras we have more than one aura. In fact we have 7 and each one of these auras can be used to pass and receive information.

Each one is of a higher vibration and each one requires a higher degree of spirituality in order to be able to pass information from and to.

It requires both the sender and the receiver to be at a similar stage of advancement before the higher auras can come into play.

The basic level of telepathy requires a certain level of spirituality before communication can work effectively, but communication via the higher auras requires ever rising levels of spirituality before it can work.

Now, the reason telepathy was mentioned was because that is the key to seeing the truth or otherwise in someone's statements.

For people who do not have sufficient spirituality to develop telepathy or have not learned how to communicate in this fashion, they are limited to just listening to the words spoken and analysing what the person is saying or, equally, observing body language in order to try to comprehend if it is truth or lies that are being spoken.

For the person who has developed telepathy, in addition to the words spoken, the body language used, the observer can receive information telepathically.

For all people, as they are thinking and speaking are sending thought information into their auras.

Not only the words they wish to share with others but some of their true thoughts coming from their minds.

Thus is the person trained in simple telepathy able to discern the truth behind the words spoken.

The point being made is that if someone has developed spirituality to the point where he can operate in his higher auras, he will instantly pick up information contained in the speaker's higher auras and instantly perceive truth or lies, for do not suppose that the higher auras contain only high levels of spirituality.

All people are constantly broadcasting using all of their auras and a trained person is able to read those auras clearly and precisely and thus understand just what the speaker is really thinking and not just what he is saying.

Thus, in the near future when enough people have been bathed in God's power coming to Earth and have developed, through prayer, meditation and service to God (service to all life) their higher auras, they will not only be able to communicate telepathically, but will also understand any hidden thoughts.

Then there can be no secrets. All will be revealed to those capable of receiving auric information.

It is not everyone who is prepared at the moment to appear naked in a spiritual sense because for so long has duplicity been considered to be the norm and we all have skeletons in our cupboards, secrets that we would prefer to keep private but, as was mentioned, we cannot progress along the path to God and spiritual freedom while we are dragging dark secrets along with us. We must be free and spiritually clean to continue along the path to God.

This is the way that the future will unfold, no more dark secrets.

Thus will the people of Earth see how their so called Elders and betters have been systematically robbing them in many domains for long ages, how vast fortunes are taken from the labors of gullible workers without a second thought for the privations imposed on workers, while this upper class amassed enormous wealth through imposing harsh taxes on hard working masses.

This system, of course, goes on to this day and few workers question why they have to pay taxes on their labors, why they have to pay taxes on the right to live somewhere, why they are taxed for every drop of water they drink and every mouthful of food they eat.

In many countries both birth and burial are also taxed.

If one was to calculate the huge amount of money collected and compare that with the amount actually spent on keeping the infrastructure of life going, one would notice a large difference. Vast amounts of money just disappear from the coffers each year.

Some of this money - indeed a lot of it - is siphoned off to keep the rich in the lifestyle to which they have been accustomed for so long and that they consider to be their due rewards for serving and guiding the lower classes.

This unfair system of robbing the poor to feed the rich will be exposed. Indeed it has already started.

People will be encouraged to work for the pleasure of serving the God-force present in their fellow man and their just reward for serving God will be the wages they receive.

Then, most of that money will be retained by them to help feed their families.

In the meantime, those who have been robbing the workers will be exposed and expelled, to be replaced by honest directors of a country.

A different system of rewarding work will be introduced.

People will be paid according to their worth to the community and not their status.

Then, for instance, those who go around collecting the rubbish of others in all weathers - variously known as trash men or dust men - will be seen to be of more service to the community than someone sitting in an air-conditioned office creating unnecessary laws. The rubbish collectors will be suitably rewarded for the service that they render to the community.

Mention must also be made of alternative energies.

A variety of alternative energy sources have been known about for a long time but have been suppressed from the public in order to keep the rich, rich at the expense of terrible damage to planet Earth.

This must and will change.

People need energy in order to heat their houses, cook their food and displace themselves, but it is no longer acceptable to rape the Earth of its life blood in order to do this.

This crime must cease.

There are, as was mentioned, a number of alternative sources of non-polluting, non-negative energies that will become available.

This will, in all probability, start with what are referred to as over unity devices that, quite simply, take the energy available in the galaxy and convert it into electricity.

Then there will be a variety of energies introduced, bit by bit, as spirituality progresses until the glorious day when pure spiritual energy will be used as a power source.

It will, in effect, be using the light force from God to power machines.

This God-force is, of course, already seen in action every time we look around us. It is the God-force that we see giving life to all things and this force can be tapped in a positive, controlled means to drive the wheels of man's industry.

But, discovering the means of using the God-force requires also that man be much more spiritually advanced than he is at the moment.
Power sources can only be discovered in the degree that man is evolved.

That is why it has taken so long to move from using beasts of burden to assist man, through using steam, coal and, now, oil, to move, soon, into primitive, but effective, over unity machines.

So you can see one's hopes, that to use pure God power to fuel machines is a long way in Earth's future.

However, let it be noted that all these proposed fuels that do not use gas, coal, oil or even sunlight or wind will be virtually free.

They will be freely available and thus must be commercialized for virtually nothing.

Once the investment to create the machines and the infrastructure of distribution recuperated, the actual fuel is free, given by the cosmos itself.

The first machines of this type have already existed for some time but have been kept secret, only available to the lucky few.

Shortly, this type of virtually free energy will be available to all and will change the world.

Perhaps one should also mention that man himself is capable, when sufficiently developed, to perform certain acts that, at the moment require machines of various types.

For instance, if a person wishes to speak to someone a long distance away, where direct speech is not possible, he requires a telephone of some kind. Sound being converted to electrical vibrations which will alternatively be picked up by another device and converted back to sound.

However, this requires electrical energy, the use of satellites and is both expensive and destructive of the planet as the source of that electrical energy is either oil or nuclear fuel.

But telepathy could easily be developed by people.

The reasons that it has not been taught are many.

Telepathy not only enables one person to communicate with another but enables that person, to a certain extent, to discern the motives behind the spoken word.

The negative beings that have for so long controlled and enslaved humanity certainly do not wish their true, dark motives to be revealed, so they teach instead, that telepathy is nonsense and is not possible to do.

Another reason for not teaching telepathy is because it would open the door to questioning how it functions. This would lead to the discovery of auras and so, eventually, the whole of accepted science would be brought into question and man would realize that he has been lied to concerning the origins of life, the makeup of life and the place of God in this maze.

The controllers of man certainly do not want mankind to wake up and question what they have been taught so, telepathy remains a myth.
One could also talk about the economic effects if mobile telephones were no longer required, but we have said enough.

Telepathy is totally possible to learn and we hope that, soon, it will be taught.

There is one other topic that we could mention that seems myth at the moment and that is teleportation. It may seem a dream to many but it is actually quite possible for man incarnate to transport himself by thought. It is the means that is used once mans incarnation is finished and he no longer has a physical body to hamper him.

However, as all is vibration, it is quite possible to manipulate the vibration, not only of the spiritual bodies (the auras) but also the physical body because that is nothing more than an aura also.

Once man develops his spirituality, not only to fill his auras with spiritual power but, by the same token, it is possible to take spiritual control of what is termed the physical body.

Should this be achieved, then all that is needed is for someone to desire to displace himself from one spot to another and he moves to that desired spot instantly.

It is not a question of travelling from one place to another but displacing oneself instantly to a desired location.

Now, it is not something that can be learned by desire, the wish to move, but it is a question of spiritual development.

This could be accomplished by anyone now but, in all probability, will be for future generations who will be more influenced by the light illuminating all of his bodies, auric, etheric and physical and thus enabling someone to develop spirituality more easily.

Thus, should teleportation be developed, the use of a vehicle would not be required.

However, like all these skills, they apply exclusively to the person concerned and thus teleportation cannot be used to transport others.
Each and every person who wishes to transport themselves by teleportation must, themselves, develop the skill.

Equally, there is a limit to what can be transported with the person.

As everything is alive, an object must itself develop the ability to teleport or they would be left behind.

It is possible for someone to 'overpower' a small inanimate object that has very little life force so that is becomes, for that moment, under the influence of the person, but a large object or an animal, for instance could not accompany anyone.

Therefore the use of teleportation is rather limited.

Nevertheless, it will become a method of personal transport in the future.

So, we will be able to communicate using telepathy and we will be able to displace ourselves using teleportation.

There will be other skills that can be developed also.

The ability to see objects or people in the dark will become possible.

The ability to move forwards and backwards in time. This will be possible because time does not exist as is imagined today. All things are occurring in what we might term the now moment so it will be a question of moving from one now moment to another.

Once again we must qualify this statement by saying that because it would be dangerous to time travel in case, by accident or intention something was altered which could affect the history of mankind, a protection exists in which the person actually travels to an alternative reality, a sort of recording of the events, either in the past or the future and even if that recording is manipulated, it will not affect the real events.

Thus, one can see that a magnificent future awaits man. A future where the slavery in which mankind lives at the moment will cease and peace, calm and freedom from any form of fear will be introduced.

This way of living was, of course, experienced a long time ago, the last time when the pendulum of time was in the bright period.

Then, gradually, the pendulum swung towards the darkness, the lack of spiritual light and Earth was plunged into the long period of tenebra.

As was previously mentioned, that dark period is now finished and the angels in heaven are singing in praise of the Lord and his light as we all, both humanity, the animals on Earth and planet Earth herself are once more bathed in the effulgent rays of pure God light.

We might, perhaps, stop to consider what happens to the opposite side of existence, when we are in light, for instance, somewhere else is in darkness and visa-versa.

We might question if there is any life on the other side of existence.

We can almost be sure that there is life everywhere so can we have any notion if there is life on the other side and what that life might look like and how it operates?

We can say with certainty that, vast distance from us, that incredible dimension that separates us from anything else there is, nevertheless life.

This life is scarcely known to us because it is so far from us and lives by rules so far removed from anything that we are familiar with that it would be difficult for us to make any intelligent comment.

But we can say that there is life. God's light always shines on some form of God's creation. God created many forms of life in his endeavour to gain experience and the life we see here on Earth, in the etheric and spiritual realms, are only a small fraction of God's creations.

God never wastes his energy so we can rest assured that whatever these life forms look like, whatever experiences they are subject to, they must, like us, go through the pendulum swing from light to dark.

If we are moving into the light, this other area must be moving into darkness and our hearts go out to them and we pray that they have the courage and strength to withstand the rigours that a long period of darkness will impose on them.

But we come out of the winter of life into God's light, so we rejoice.

We look forward to life unfolding much as we have predicted, man, animals and planet Earth all starting to shine with God's power.

We know, approximately, what will occur thanks to the recollections of the wonderful, wise people who lived that last light period and recounted events to us.

We are a long way from the maximum point of freedom from Archon slavery but each and every day draws us further into the light.

Each and everyday draws us closer to the elimination of Archon control and will bring us, eventually, into a period that no one incarnate at the moment could imagine.

Love for all, love for oneself, freedom from any form of fear.

Amazing forms of energy released into our grasp, eliminating any form of poverty and by the same token, eliminating any need for war, migrations and jealousy between the haves and the have not's. We will all have equally.

This and more is the destiny of man as we progress through the light filled millennia.

Peace and total freedom for all.

CHAPTER FIVE

LIFE IN LIGHT

The revelation of a different way of living: peace, love and harmony, instead of conflict, hate and competition will take a long time to be accepted by the majority of the world's population, so do not think that what we have mentioned as inevitable progress into light will occur straight away.

Life changes slowly.

We must accept that the majority of the humans incarnate at the moment have no idea of the spiritual changes happening and so continue on their daily round as lost as they were before the solar system started to move into the light.

It is true that many children are being born at the moment incarnate with that knowledge installed in them, but it is also true that the evil ones are aware of this and have installed a system of injecting newborns babies with poisons in the hopes of preventing them from realizing their potentials.

This is a terrible crime and the perpetrators will pay heavily for the harm they are causing to beautiful children who could have helped push the knowledge of spirituality forward but, instead, find themselves isolated in a world that is cut off from our world.

Nevertheless, as has been mentioned, nothing will prevent life from unfolding in the future as has been predicted.

This prediction is based upon the way things unfolded long ago, the last time the galaxy moved into the light and so it will happen again in much the same way.

Life always moves in circles and those wise beings who lived through those events long ago have reported to us how events unfolded.

However, we cannot be sure that life this time will be a carbon copy of the unfolding last time, but we can be sure of how the main events will be revealed this time.

It is a wonderful time to be living in and the heavenly hosts are rejoicing that life is moving into these joyous times.

It is important that we all, both those incarnate and those discarnate act together in as positive a fashion as possible.

We mentioned in the last chapter how the light from God will illuminate every corner of creation chasing darkness and replacing it with God's power.

We wish now to jump forward a long time into the future and explain how we expect life on planet Earth to appear.

It must be clearly understood that light, as we now see it, is not at all how light really is.

Light is the power of God - the God-force.

But, light is life.

More than this, light is a living substance that has remarkable elements to it.

One of these elements is of a crystalline nature.

If we examine the stones that we call crystals and compare them with ordinary rocks and stones we can get some idea of the difference.
Stones are dense, cold, apparently lifeless objects, although they do contain a life force.

But crystals can be seen as things of great beauty, translucent or transparent. Either clear like glass or of great beauty: pink, blue, green and of many colors.

These crystals are, in fact, remnants of stones remaining from the last time Earth was bathed by the God-force.

During the long ages that Earth was in spiritual darkness, what we know as stones and rocks have been formed, a reflection of the darkness, the lack of spirituality that has been formed on the surface of the planet, and on other planets and moons also.

But, deep underground, can still be found the beautiful stones we call crystals that formed long ago through the God light shining on the surface. They have been covered by more modern formations as the planets grow over the long ages.

Therefore, it is expected that long into the future the surface of planet Earth and other planets and astral bodies will once again, glow and scintillate as the God-force creates more crystals, but that will be lying on the surface.

This will be the natural result of the rising in spirituality of all life in response to the God-force, of a much higher frequency causing beauty to be formed everywhere.

Planet Earth will become a thing of incredible beauty, truly a joy to live on.

It will, in fact, become the Garden of Eden described in the Bible, although humanity will not be wandering about naked and in ignorance as is described in the Old Testament.

Quite the opposite will obtain.

Man will not need clothes quite as they are known at the moment. Humanity will, through an act of 'will' be able to create whatever form of garment he wishes to clothe him.

Last time we were in this blessed state, the majority of people clothed themselves in garments of a rainbow hue, garments, not created from things of the Earth: animal or vegetable, but raiment's created from their minds. As minds were pure and full of beauty, so the clothes they summoned were also things of beauty constructed from astral energy.

It was similar with housing. It was no longer necessary to pillage the Earth of its minerals to build houses. They were created from astral matter by an act of will.

These remarkable acts are possible through the rising of consciousness to the point that manipulation of energy becomes possible.

It sounds like science fiction at the moment, and would, certainly, be almost impossible but times change and, once the move into the light truly occurs and, once mankind, bathed in this light, realizes his potential, virtually nothing will be impossible.

The God-force has no limit and so, people filled with this God-force will also know, virtually, no limit, only the limit that people impose upon themselves according to their level of spirituality.

Naturally, by this time the power of the Archons will have been totally removed as will have been any influence by the psychotic people who, at the moment, run your world.

Wars will have long since ceased.

Consumption of animal flesh and by products will have stopped.
Most animals will have lost their fear of man and we (man and beast) will live in peace together.

So we present a picture of a planet Earth totally healed, loved and respected, glowing with the spiritual God-force present in all its elements: stones, plants and water, man dressed in rainbow colored robes and the whole world living in peace.

This glorious image will become reality and will gradually become so, from the humble beginnings we have today to its peak of perfection before, inevitably, declining back to what we now see.

This is the inevitable, unstoppable swing of the pendulum of life, back and forth between growth and returning it to its source - God.

But, at the moment, we are in the spring of this event so we can look forward to a long, long summer before autumn sets in and we return to the winter of existence.

This positive phase will exist for many hundreds of thousands of years so let us rejoice in the glory that is coming to us.

We must now look to our more immediate future, when life will not have reached its climax, but nevertheless, is not as dismal as it is at the moment.

What can we expect to see?

Once again, thanks to the memories of the wise ones who had incarnations at that time and were willing to share their memories with us, we can make an estimate of this probable future.

The first thing that should happen, as has been mentioned previously, the evil ones who run the planet will be exposed and removed from power.

We repeat for anyone who has not read the previous chapters, the time of the Archons, their stranglehold on all life on Earth and the time of their psychopathic minions is over.

Life will have difficulty in changing until the hold on the reality that they have created is removed.

That time is already upon us. The next few years will see great change, great freedom come to Earth.

As soon as their domination is removed, then we will see zero-point energy introduced.

This as has, once again, been mentioned previously, will provide virtually free electrical energy for all the world.

Zero-point energy quite simply takes the differential energy from what we refer to as the sky and the planet Earth and that energy can be converted into electrical power.

This differential energy is similar to what is observed during a thunderstorm when huge amounts of this power are unleashed in a somewhat uncontrolled fashion.

But it gives a clear indication of the energy available. Man is able to tap into this energy and release it in a controlled fashion providing endless, unlimited energy for man to use.

There is no limit to this power.

It exists, quite simply because of the differential in spiritual power between the sky and the Earth, a differential that it is always trying to balance.

So, by capturing some of this differential it will be possible to provide energy for all to use.

Now, we must consider a form of transport that already exists but has been kept out of the public domain for many years. We refer to anti-gravity transport.

For long ages, man has noticed strange craft crossing the skies and has questioned how they flew: silently, and incredible speeds and not observing the laws of physics that science is used to following.

There are a number of forms of locomotion of these various flying craft but some of them use zero-point energy.

This energy can be tapped by devices standing on the surface of the Earth but can also be captured by craft in the skies.

This energy, which is basically vibration can be manipulated to provide a power that is termed 'anti-gravity'.

It is perhaps not the moment to go into a lesson on advanced, alternative physics but we will say that vibration can be manipulated to provide an attractive force or a repelling force.

The power that is termed gravity is a power, a force, that has not been understood by general science. Indeed it is a subject that has been deliberately kept from the public eye because an understanding of how gravity works would open the door to understanding both free energy - zero point energy - but also help people to develop anti-gravity machines.

However, as spiritual light floods all of creation so all must be revealed.

The secret of zero-point energy will be revealed as will how anti-gravity works be released to the public domain.

Thus we can expect to see more objects flying through the skies, much as we have airplanes at the moment but these new forms of flying transport will be silent, swift and harmless to the Earth.

Once again, this may seem to be science fiction at the moment but it is a form of transport already being used by certain military groups but it has been kept from the public eye as much as possible in order, amongst other reasons, to enable certain rich people to become even more rich at the expense of planet Earth, as oil, water and other elements play a part in the health of the planet.

Once zero-point energy becomes freely available to all, of course much will change.

We break off here in our discussion of the ascent of man to discuss something that we have been reluctant to discuss because it would have caused turmoil and fear if we had mentioned it years ago and that is the beings that are also seen in the skies at the moment flying in unusual shaped craft silently and clearly using out of this world technology.

We refer to what we call aliens.

This group, or rather, these groups of beings, come from various dimensions and areas of life far removed from planet Earth and its apparent solidity.

It must be said that there are life forms also present on Earth that look human but that come from what we term a different dimension.

Now, there are dimensions that are of such a different vibrational frequency that the beings that live there would be invisible to the untrained eye but there are also dimensions, if we can call them such, that vibrate at a slightly different frequency from your 3D world.
In those dimensions, and there are a number of them, beings of all sorts live.

Some are totally visible to us, some are translucent and some, of course invisible.

Among all those different beings we find the nature spirits: gnomes, elves and so on. On slightly higher frequencies we find the fairy folk who have the ability, along with the nature spirits to raise or lower their frequencies to make themselves either visible or invisible to the human eye.

The raising or lowering of frequency also enables them to alter their degree of solidity in relation to our material world.

Thus, in a visible state, these beings may have a degree of solidity very much like our dimension. But, as they raise their frequency, they not only are able to move in degrees if required between visible and invisible but, in the same degree, can alter their degree of solidity, being able to move through what appears to be solid walls.

These almost magical, to our eyes, feats - moving from visible to invisible and passing through solid objects - is not magical at all. It is simply a question of changing frequency rather as if someone was tapping on the keys of a piano, moving up or down the scale.

Humanity will, one day, far into the future be able to accomplish these feats. Indeed mankind already has the capability but has not developed his spiritual awareness to be able to put this into practice.

So, to return to these human like beings that share the planet Earth with us, we could call them a different parallel branch that have existed for at least as long as humanity has but have not been subject to the rise and fall of life that has been described earlier.

Their evolution has followed a different path to we humans and thus have had different events happening to them, events that have been less dramatic and negative to their progress.

We, who also live in the astral realms have little contact with them, being first and foremost concerned with the evolution of humans on Earth and in our astral realms, but our paths do cross from time to time and we do communicate with them.

So to repeat for the sake of clarity, there exists this race of beings that have a parallel evolution to us, are much more spiritually evolved than most of the human race currently occupying planet Earth and that tend to keep to themselves. Until now.

They have started to make themselves more visible to us because the actions of man with his destructive intentions is interfering with the planet and thus, is interfering with them.

The mining and other actions done by man in the past caused little interference with them but the more recent activities: nuclear explosions and what is termed Fracking is not only harming the planet but is also of great concern to this race of people.

Thus, they have made themselves known to some of the leaders of certain developed countries and have tried to explain the changes and the harm that is being caused by man's ill-advised actions.

As is well known, the greed of man and his war like actions resulted in the refusal of our leaders, both military and political, to listen to these people and to heed their advice. But our concern, at the moment, is not with the stupidity of man, but on an investigation of the human like forms that live on the planet Earth and in her astral realms.

So we will describe these beings, what they look like and how they live as far as is known.

Physically, they resemble man to a large degree.

They tend to be tall, slim, with silver hair and would be considered 'good looking' although some of their good looks is the result of their high level of spirituality shining from them and affecting people's impression of them.

They are of the two sexes, like man, male and female. They fecund in a similar way to man and have children.

They have long lives compared to man, partly because of their peaceful, stress-less way of living and partly because spirituality tends to help in the prolongation of physical life.

To describe their homes is difficult because they have developed the ability to be physical and nonphysical.

When physical, they tend to live deep underground in caverns that they have terra-formed according to their needs.

When in non-physical form, of course, they need no home, being pure spirit.

Their food is simple. They are vegan and eat little, drawing much of their sustenance from the auric fields surrounding the planet.

When alone, they are able to transport themselves by teleportation.
When in groups they use craft that you would term space ships, the propulsion system being a modified zero-point energy machine, modified by mixing a spiritual element with the physical machine, a system a long way in the future for man.

They communicate telepathically. Thus they can not only communicate with each other but can communicate with us.

Telepathy is a universal language.

Let us now turn to think about other life forms that are visiting planet Earth at the moment and, indeed have been doing so for long ages.
It has been mentioned that this planet (Earth) is the only one in the galaxy with life in the physical form on the surface.

This unique fact has been the cause of great interest to many life forms that, themselves, live in astral realms but desire to explore life in physical form.

Thus, they have a problem. Being made of astral material these beings are not able to visit Earth in a physical form without a great deal of artificial assistance.

Also, being astral in form, they are immortal and so have had immense amounts of time to resolve their problems.

The problems are many and complex.

The major problem to overcome is, first and foremost, how to visit planet Earth from their auric homes.

Everything is made of vibration, frequency.

So, regardless of the level of spirituality in a Godly sense, the auric fields are of a higher frequency than life on planet Earth.

So it was necessary to find a means of reducing their frequency, both in a singular and in a collective sense to match the frequency of planet Earth.

It is a question of bombarding the individual or groups of individuals with the frequency of what is termed the third dimension and that enables a change to occur in the form of the being under discussion so that he can match the frequency of planet Earth and with our galaxy.

Once this is achieved the being or beings are in a position to assume a sort of physicality at least temporarily.

However, they would still be distant from planet Earth because it is not sufficient to match the carrier wave frequency of this dimension. It requires also knowing the exact frequency of the place either on Earth or on another planet that they might wish to visit.

The subject of each point in our galaxy having a unique frequency has also been previously discussed.

So they would not only need to bombard themselves with the carrier wave frequency of the third dimension but also of the frequency of the exact spot that they wish to visit.

Having successfully achieved this they would disappear from their auric home and arrive at their destination here on planet Earth or on one of the many planets or moons that are in our solar system.

So they would arrive somewhere and have a sort of temporary physical form but would not have the means of operating successfully on the surface of a planet.

To operate correctly in physicality requires a great deal more that just a physical form.

It requires clothing, food suitable for the being who is going to consume it.

It also requires a suitable temperature, light conditions among many other needs.

So the problems go on and on.

Let us recapitulate.

Beings in astral form from a certain dimension needed to learn how to alter their quiescent frequency, from their basic frequency to that of our physical dimension.

Then they needed to learn how to project to the spot in our universe where they wanted to appear.

Also, as was just mentioned they needed to create a body that could survive on the particular planet they wished to visit.

Some things it was possible to master and other things proved impossible.

Strangely enough the things that humans would consider the most difficult - the changing of frequencies and the ability to arrive at a particular spot - was the easiest for many races of aliens.

This is because many of these groups have science very developed and so the knowledge of how to manipulate frequencies was well known to them.

The real challenge to them was to create a body suitable for living on any particular planet.

This was new to them so they had no knowledge to fall back on.

So they were obliged to abandon that idea.

But they did not abandon the idea of visiting planet Earth.

Thus they developed robotic entities that they could send to Earth to harvest materials that could be used to create a more long lasting form of robot capable of successfully operating on Earth.

Now, before we go on with this history lesson we must mention the means of transport variously known as flying saucers, UFOs, etc.
Remember that these aliens all live in the astral realms so do not have any physicality.

It was mentioned previously that teleportation is possible but that one could not do it in a group fashion, nor could large amounts of material be transported.

Thus to harvest materials from Earth and to transport them to an astral world, some means of container needed to be manufactured.

Thus, over time, in astral form, various forms of flying machines were invented by the diverse races.

As was mentioned, most of these races have a firm foundation in science, so it was relatively easy for them to fabricate, in astral form, flying machines that could, themselves, not only transport beings (robots) and materials, but could be altered in their quiescent frequency to operate in our dimension.

According to the race building these machines, they have different shapes and their power source is different.

But they all use a form of anti-gravity as that was considered to be a requirement so that they were independent of the need to use fossil fuels or any other primitive power source.

We should also mention that these flying craft were constructed with a high source of intelligence compared to anything known on Earth, to the point they could be considered alive, even if it is an artificial intelligence form of life.

So these flying machines can think for themselves, calculate the course that they need to take and much more.

Now, the robotic creatures, known to the military as EBE's. EXTRATERRESTRIAL BIOLOGICAL ENTITY'S were sent to Earth to gather materials that were hoped to be suitable for creating a more enduring form of artificial intelligence.

This is where things become almost laughable from a human standpoint.

These robots, were instructed to gather a variety of plants, animals, fish and even humans.

Then the frequency was altered up to the quiescent frequency of the astral realm concerned at which point attempts were made to construct viable creatures.

After much experimentation a small robot was constructed, partly out of vegetable matter, with a skin of modified Dolphin skin and with a modified human brain.

It's basic shape was also humanoid.

It is the being known as the Grey.

We must remember that this creature was first constructed in astral realms but was found to work effectively in our dimension.

The mental component - artificial intelligence - is sufficient to obey commands and also perform acts that mystify us - levitation, teleportation and the ability to pass through apparently solid objects - but is, nevertheless, just sufficiently intelligent to obey orders.

This almost comical little creature has become a standard working model for many alien groups that still remain hidden from our eyes in the astral realms.

We should mention also the strange looking entities sometimes known as Praying Mantis.

Once again they are a construct, an artificial intelligence object created from Earthly matter.

Quite why a Praying Mantis form of a creature was copied we don't know for sure.

It is possible that it is sufficiently human like in its bodily make up to fill the requirements of the aliens looking to emulate life here on Earth.

Certainly, it has a distinct head, two eyes and other facial features, a body, two arms and two legs. It also can stand upright in a similar fashion to man so, perhaps it was a good choice.

In any case, these artificial beings were constructed and found to be successful at being able to operate on Earth.

Generally, it seems that they are given a higher degree of intelligence than the Grey robots but, nevertheless, are just robots obeying the wishes of their masters, the aliens living in the astral realms.

The instructions are given both to the space ships (when required) and also to the EBE's telepathically.

Mention has been made of the Draco's, but these are of the Archon construct and do not enter into this discussion.

There have also come onto the scene in recent years a variety of other alien creatures.

Some of these are more recent robotic constructs, some astral projections (holograms) and some of them implanted images put into the minds of people.

In no case are they real aliens as none have found a way of living on planet Earth.

This, of course takes us into the unpleasant subject of abductions both of humans and animals and is the prime reason that we were reluctant to talk about the alien subject at all.

However, times change and no discussion about the human race would be complete if we did not mention the alien intervention and interference of humanity by aliens.

People claim to be abducted by the Grey robots, taken into space ships, or facilities somewhere and undergo very unpleasant examinations. They are also shown vaguely human looking fetuses grown in giant test tubes.

Further the victims of these abductions claim to be shown strange looking children and are informed that the child was constructed from their genetic material - sperm or ova.

Now, some of these stories are mental hallucinations. Many are implanted images done to observe the reactions of people without going to the actual trouble of performing all these acts, but some, it is sad to say, seem to be based on actual abduction and experimentation.

The object, when it occurs, quite simply, is to try to produce a viable human body, capable of surviving on Earth, but with a brain linked to the alien's brains rather as is done with the robots, so that these human looking beings could have the alien, in his astral world, nevertheless experiencing life here on Earth.

These beings are generally called hybrids.

Now, all things are alive. So the sperm and ova used to create the body that grew in a test tube is alive but there is more to successfully living than just being alive.

A real human is a complex being with many parts to his make up, much of it spiritual in nature.

The beings that the aliens grow in test tubes, if left to develop naturally, would become normal human beings, the result of a sexual joining of sperm and ova.

But this is not what the aliens desire.

They seek to have a human but with an enslaved mind, a sort of artificial intelligence that they, the aliens, can command and that the hybrid would obey without question.

Real humans tend to think for themselves which is not what the aliens want at all.

So they alter the brain of the hybrid.

We are calling them hybrids for the sake of not confusing them with true humans although they are not hybrids really, have been made from human genetics.

Now, they alter the brain to try and install an artificial intelligence element into it.

Without exception, up until now, it has not worked.

The human body rejects the interference and so the unfortunate hybrid becomes ill after a while and is destroyed.

Before we leave the topic of aliens and move on to other areas of interest we need to round off the subject.

We have mentioned in earlier chapters the psychopathic leaders of planet Earth, humans under the control of Archons who have only their best interests at heart. That of the Archons.

For the sake of clarity we will repeat that Archons are non-physical beings and have been considered to be an artificial intelligence life form, although that is not entirely true.

It would be closer to reality if we considered them to be more like ants and bees.

They have a hierarchy of sorts and a strict code of discipline.

The military groups around the world are based on Archon principals.

This is where things start to get complex.

We have mentioned a variety of different life forms that have either visited the planet Earth or who have attempted to do so.

We have also mentioned this parallel human life that has shared Earth with man for long ages and who have remained apart from mankind generally speaking.

We must touch on motives.

If beings decide to expend large amounts of energy to go from one place to another, there is usually a reason for this.

In some cases it is simple curiosity.

In others it is to learn how to create physical form but in many cases it is in the hope of getting some advantage: spiritual, material or for power motives.

In the case of the Archons, as was explained, it was for power, domination, even a form of evil.

There are other groups of aliens who are not far removed from the Archons in outlook.

The human military machine, being under the control of psychopaths and thus under the control of Archons naturally attracted the attention of similar minded aliens and so very quickly found a common ground from which to work.

Thus, very quickly, an exchange system was set up. These alien groups gave the human military what they sought - advanced negative energy sources that could be converted into weapons of various sorts and, in exchange, the military gave these aliens carte blanche, via their different robots, to live on planet Earth and to conduct their various experiments in the vain hopes of achieving their goal - to be able to live on Earth.

Of course, all this has its limits in both senses.

The military have indeed manufactured flying machines and various other technologies that were taught to them by aliens but, not having the skill of the aliens, can only make poor copies of true alien technology whilst, at the same time, the aliens have not yet produced viable hybrids.

But, fortunately, there are other groups of alien life forms with more noble, peaceful, ambitions and whom we might consider to be, not exactly guardians of planet Earth, but certainly have our best interests at heart rather as, in the case of humans, there are some who exploit animals and some who take it upon themselves to protect animals.

We have described the two extremes: aliens that we might consider negative and aliens that we might consider positive.

As with all life, apart from these extremes there are a number of groups that visit Earth with other motives but we have gone to some length to explain why the skies contain flying machines and why the robots that pilot them, and that interact with man, do so.

But we must not forget the pendulum swing of life that was described in earlier descriptions of life.

Much of what we described, and we break off for a moment to say that alien visitation of Earth goes back a long way into the past, was only possible because the galaxy was passing through the negative aspect of life.

Now, of course, the galaxy is rapidly moving into the light filled aspect.

Thus, great changes will occur in the galaxy at large and in planet Earth in particular.

We mention that the time of the Archons and of their psychopathic minions is drawing to a close.

Therefore, wars will eventually cease.

As there will be no need of armies, the military that are working with these negative aliens will be disbanded. Then the public will start to discover the full extent of the harm created to some humans and aliens by these robots.

They will be disposed of and contact with the negative aliens will cease.

However, contact with the positive aliens will be encouraged and, as man develops the ability to use telepathy, direct contact with these good beings will occur.

Thus they will share their advanced, peaceful knowledge with us and thus will man progress more quickly.

Spirituality does not preclude advanced technology. Indeed, they can advance together so, as man advances in spirituality, so advanced peaceful technology will be shared with us by these peaceful aliens.

We will begin exchange programs with them, not necessarily in terms of visiting each other, although this will eventually be possible, but exchange of ideas and concepts to permit man to advance towards perfection more quickly.

So, like all life, the dark times are fading and man and his space brothers will move into the light together for, do not forget, that even the more advanced alien life has been battling the powers of darkness and are themselves celebrating moving into the light.

CHAPTER SIX

MOVING HOUSE

When we do anything that has any real significance in our lives a number of events must occur.

We are so used to doing things that we seldom really stop to consider the events taking place and yet life is always following a similar course.

For instance, we have discussed previously the life cycle of virtually everything: from birth to growth, to decline and to, finally, what is termed death, although, of course nothing can die.

It seems normal for us to experience this because man, incarnate, experiences it all the time. We are surrounded by people giving birth, the baby growing from infancy into adulthood, becoming old and finally dying.

So we seldom stop to consider why this should occur.

We observe a similar event if we watch the unfolding of the four seasons of a year: spring, summer, autumn and winter.

How many people have stopped to compare these four seasons to the incarnation cycle of living beings?

And yet the life cycle of virtually everything follows the same pattern: birth, growth, decline and death.

If we had the means to step outside of time and could observe the life cycle of a planet or, indeed, a galaxy, we would observe the same pattern.

We can't imagine a planet or a galaxy being born, growing old and eventually dying, but it is the inevitable cycle that all life goes through.

The planet Earth, for example, we assume was always here and always will be. But there was a time when it didn't exist.

So how did it come into being?

This subject has been discussed before but we mention it again because, to understand these life cycles will help us understand more about who God is, what the intentions of this force we call God are and what our place in God's plans is.

So let us imagine a time when planet Earth did not exist.

Nothing can appear out of the blue, like magic, so something created the planet Earth.

To understand somewhat the process that resulted in the formation - the birth - of the planet, it will be relevant to follow the process that creates a living entity: a baby mammal, an insect, a fish or whatever.

The process starts with the desire to create a new life.

In the case of humans who live together in matrimonial form, one or both of the couple have the desire to 'start a family' as it is called.

Long before that happy moment, the desire of people to live together, so that a sexual union can occur, is happening and it is this desire to procreate that is at the base of this creative act.

Of course, even in what is called 'rape' there is the desire of one person to have what is termed 'sex'.

Now, we can see that the creative act starts with a thought, a desire to produce something, a baby, in the case of mammals and insects.

Even plants have this desire to produce an offspring.

So can we assume that behind the creation of a planet or even a galaxy is a desire to create?

If this is so, then there must be an intelligence that causes a planet or galaxy to appear.

What is this intelligence?

We have already mentioned a mysterious force that we call God.

We have tried to explain that no one knows where this force came from but we have also explained that this force - God - is alive and has self awareness.

We went on, earlier, to explain that God decided in its desire to understand what it is, that it created, over vast eons of time, all that now exists.

Further, we explained that God created eight bands of different frequency, eight carrier waves that would, ultimately, have life on them and we talked about God creating planets in astral form on the eighth and the seventh planes or dimensions.

We must stress that these planets are not physical but astral. They could be considered to be thought forms, the product of the thoughts of God in his desire, his curiosity, to explore the limits that life could go to as it, too, explored the astral realms.

However, we stopped after we had mentioned the eighth and seventh dimensions and discussed other topics.

But, those who are themselves interested in esoteric matters, will know that there remain six more planes of vibration to consider.

So let us now return to the sixth plane and try to find out why it exists and why life is on it.

The sixth plane of vibration corresponds to a certain part of the makeup of man.
We should point out at this time that when we speak of man we are not only describing humanity as it is thought of by the people we observe on Earth, but also human-like entities that are in the astral realms and whose make-up follows, vaguely, humanity.
We refer to some of the alien groups that are starting to influence life now. But humanity, being a complex multi-layered creature, cannot just be formed as one homogeneous entity. A large part of the makeup of man is spiritual as opposed to physical and a large part of that lives, if we may use that word, on various carrier waves of existence created by God all those long years ago.
So, part of man lives on the sixth plane.
The questions is, which part?

We have mentioned that man uses a number of facilities in his attempt to capture the God-force.
The one that is based on the sixth plane is imagination.
The fact that imagination is based on such a high plane, the sixth, should give some idea of how important imagination is in the make-up, the construction, of man.
Imagination is closely connected to the higher self (higher mind) and can work in conjunction with higher mind in a developed person.
Earlier, we described the eighth plane and the seventh plane and tried to explain what is to be observed on those planes of reality.
Can we describe the sixth plane?

The problem is that there is nothing to see in an astral, physical, sense. No planets, no life forms, nothing that man incarnate could identify with.
However, this imagination resides there.
The imagination is, itself, difficult to describe because we all have imagination and yet there is only one imagination as there is actually only one life force - God. So it is the imagination of God that resides there.
Who amongst us could understand this concept? Not many, we suggest and yet we need imagination to 'imagine' what imagination is.
Can you see the conundrum?

We need imagination to visualize what imagination is but we also need to be able to imagine just how it can be that there is only one imagination.
So the best we can say that the sixth plane is a storehouse of imagination and that we all, as individual consciousnesses, can tap into that storehouse to take some of it when needed.
Therefore, depending on the degree of development of our imagination, we are more or less in touch with that plane - the sixth.

Now imagination needs to be used carefully. It was mentioned in another talk that a developed imagination working in conjunction with our higher mind can produce amazing results.
Equally a developed imagination working in an unbridled sense can produce nonsense.
We have heard of people imagining all sorts of things that do not and could not exist in any form of reality but, to the person under the influence of this uncontrolled imagination, seems real.
Mental institutions all over the world are full of people under the control of unbridled imagination and these unfortunate people live a very sad life as they are swung about in all directions under the impulse of their imagination.
These people are totally convinced that what they create with their imagination is absolutely real and it is very hard to cure such people.
Further, as imagination is part of the spiritual makeup of man, it can follow them into the afterlife and there are hospital areas in what is called heaven devoted to trying to cure such people from the domination of imagination out of control.

It is true to say that none of us - or very few - are totally free of the effects of imagination creating illusion and it is one of the disciplines that the spiritual path tries to correct, ensuring that imagination is based in reality and not in illusion.
And yet, imagination is part of the God-force and it is unreasonable to think of God as having a mental condition that would require psychiatric treatment!
So, if God is completely sane and the imagination found in the sixth plane is that of God, why should anyone who is tapping into that one God imagination be out of control and require treatment?

The answer is consciousness.

We all have individual consciousness, as has been mentioned. This consciousness is, itself, able to think, calculate and reason but this consciousness has no means of knowing that what it is thinking about is true or false.

Consciousness is the force that helps us create our reality but, of itself, has no means to analyse what it is creating.

The idea that God created, when he created man, was for all mankind to be in touch with the higher self (higher mind).

If and when this happens of course, there can be no falsehood because higher mind is God itself and this must be totally sane.

But, the Archons realized this fact long years ago and so discouraged mankind from contacting their higher mind by creating religions that forbid people from doing meditation and from any action that would promulgate contact with the higher mind.

So, imagination, which should be in contact with both the higher mind and consciousness, acting as a bridge between higher mind and consciousness, does not do this and so consciousness is left to wander about influenced by imagination, which itself, is not being guided by higher mind.

Thus, perhaps you can see that the consciousness of many people is completely lost as is imagination.

This was the intention of the Archons who can step in, in place of higher mind, and influence people's imagination and consciousness, not in a positive manner but negatively, pushing people to act in the strange manner that they do at the moment and have done for many millennia. Creating a topsy turvy world where sanity is suppressed and lunacy takes its place.

This upside-down world in which so many people live has been in place for so long that it is considered by many, indeed most, to be perfectly normal.

We will not bother to give any examples as a complete list of this craziness would fill an entire book.

Sufficient to say that, when a person starts to be able to think and act in a sane manner, that person would have to adjust every aspect of their life in order to get it back on track.

The good news is, of course, that, as we have mentioned time and again, the time of the Archons is drawing to a close and people will start to wake up to a reality based on truth and not on lies.

So let us examine what this truth might look like when seen through the higher self (higher mind).

The first thing is to realize that truth is a comparative program based on past experience and on belief systems. In other words, there is no one truth but that does not mean that people have to use lies in place of truth.

But it does imply that we all have our own version of truth that is applicable exclusively to us.

It also implies that it would be incorrect to oblige another person to accept our version of truth when that person knows perfectly well that what we are expounding does not coincide with their beliefs and experiences at all.

The great masters like Jesus understood this very well and advised us not to force others to live by our rules.

The next thing that we should realize is that the law of mutual attraction is always at work and thus, if we believe something to be true, we can always find others like minded. Thus, if sufficient people think the same thing, it becomes accepted as truth and anyone who does not agree with that point of view is ostracized from society.

It is in this fashion that religions, laws and standards of general behaviours are created to which all must comply.

It must be said that if it curbs the excesses of negative behaviour from a person or group, it is beneficial but, if, for example, it promulgates nonsense concerning physics or nature it is not very helpful.

Indeed the incorrect understanding of the way life is constructed, encouraged by those under the influence of the Archons, has acted as a brake to the development of science for many long ages.

So, is there a way actually of finding truth?

There is and it is revealed in the degree that we can contact higher mind.

It was mentioned that God presented man with countless problems years ago and the solutions to those problems found by early, astral man, were fed into the God-force.

Thus we can assume that God knows the truth about all subjects.

Further, God is also our higher mind and so our higher mind must have access to truth.

This is where the sixth plane comes into play.

The sixth plane is the plane of imagination. But, in the construction of man, we find various areas that were designed to work together to allow man to realize who and what God is and imagination plays a pivotal role in this process.

At one end of the construction of man we find the higher self. At the extreme other end is physical brain.

There is a long chain of different parts to the makeup of man that should, if they are all working together correctly, feed truth from the higher mind into the brain so that any necessary action can occur.

Next, in the chain from the higher mind is imagination. All truth issued on any subject by the higher mind must pass through imagination before being passed onto the next level.

This is why imagination has been given such an important place in the construction of the eight carrier waves that God originally created.

Now, what exactly is the role of imagination in disseminating wisdom to the brain?

The higher mind thinks in terms of pure thought, pure concepts. But the brain is at home using images of various sorts: either words, which are images, mathematics, which are other images or pictures.

So, the function of imagination is to translate these pure thoughts coming from the higher mind into words, images or pictures that the brain is familiar with and can put into practice if required.

The problem is that imagination has intelligence and can think for itself. It can create its own words, images and pictures and often does.

Indeed, for most people who have not developed the ability to contact their higher mind, their imagination is all they have to help them resolve problems and find answers.

But imagination, divorced from contact and direction from the higher mind, is rather like a ship without a rudder to steer it.

So it pushes the brain of the person concerned to bob about in a stormy sea of astral and etheric thoughts with no hope of gaining control of its destination.

The answer to the problem is to make contact with the higher mind.

This can be achieved through meditation but even then it takes a lot of spiritual training to persuade imagination to work in conjunction with, and under the control of, higher mind.

Imagination, so used to thinking for itself, is not used to being the servant of higher mind and it takes much dedication to the spiritual path to teach it to stop thinking for itself and to obey the directions of higher mind.

But it can be achieved and then, as was mentioned earlier, the person working with higher mind and imagination together becomes a powerful person indeed.

However, the majority of people do not need to become spiritual or mental giants and so, the imagination does not need to be developed to the highest degree.

The higher mind contains nothing but truth and so any information projected from higher mind is total reality, without any nuance.

This is where imagination comes into play.

In a really developed person, the imagination is fully open and so truth from the higher mind flows into the physical brain undiminished.

This could, and would, cause problems for many people living in a world consisting mainly of falsehoods while their outlook on life would be at total variance to that world.

This has been the trouble that many advanced beings experienced when they found themselves expressing one point of view when the rest of their nation believed something virtually the opposite.

We should avoid this at all costs.

Life on Earth is difficult enough without expressing an opinion that no one else is advanced enough to accept.

Therefore we need to allow imagination to act as a filter of truth.

This can happen more or less automatically if we control our imagination.

Through meditation, imagination becomes, gradually, more open, allowing a certain amount of truth from the higher mind to filter through.

The student will start to compare the new information filling his mind with information accepted by the general public.

Should he express, when talking to his friends or family, that opinions he expresses is more or less accepted by his comrades, he is on safe ground and is rendering service by pushing knowledge along towards truth but, should he

say something that is instantly rejected by others, he should accept that he has passed the barrier of what he should and should not say.
Thus, the student could, perhaps, stop developing his imagination for a while to allow the rest of society to catch up with him or, at least, refrain from mentioning certain things.

It is possible to meditate and develop other faculties without, necessarily, opening the door of imagination too fast.
These other faculties have already been mentioned. They are called gifts of the spirit: clairaudience, telekinesis, clairvoyance, etc.
However, the student should avoid mentioned these gifts and certainly should not demonstrate them except to aid others in difficulty.
Gifts of the spirit come, primarily, from God, and God rewards his servants in many ways but God also reserves the right to remove his gifts from anyone who abuses them.

Let us turn to another aspect of imagination often ignored and that is the way art is used to influence people. We say ignored because the general public, when looking at art, observe the finished effect: a painting, a film or whatever and seldom question from whence the skill to create all this came from.
It has been said that genius is ten percent inspiration and ninety percent perspiration and this may be true but, without the ten percent inspiration nothing artistic would be created.
If one questions a true artist, they often admit that they do not know where the original idea came from. It just appeared in their mind, one day.
We have previously stated that nothing can appear like magic, out of the blue, and so there must be a place where that idea was stored and there must have been a mechanism that allowed it to be released, to become reality after much hard work.

Now, we have mentioned 'brain'. And yet brain is just a flesh and blood organ, operating by electricity and controlling the body.
Thus, genius cannot come from that.
Working in close association with brain is a spiritual equivalent of brain called 'mind'.
The function of mind is to tell brain to operate the elements of the body via the aforementioned electrical impulses.
Therefore genius cannot originate in the mind.

So where is this storehouse of amazing thoughts we call genius?
It cannot even be the higher mind that contains all knowledge, but genius, by its very concept, is creating something original that does not exist anywhere.

Genius is to be found in the I.D.

The ID is a unique, meaning one, form of consciousness.
There is only one ID and it is present, or rather, available, to all.
It is the basic pattern, form, around which human life, in all its shapes and no matter what dimension it lives in, contains.
There is just one ID.
It is not life - God is life.
It is separate from higher mind and from all the various spiritual and astral parts that go to make-up man.
The ID is different and apart from all these things.
It is not even collective conscious although it closely resembles it and it certainly is not individual consciousness.
It is a unique oneness that joins all humans together in a way that even God does not, although we must recognise that ID was a construct of God.
So every single person, in no matter what dimension they live, physical or astral, shares the same, one ID.

What is the purpose of ID?
As was mentioned, all is one and yet it is clear that man is not an animal nor something mineral.
God created all life. But the purpose of the ID is to create the archetypal form of man to delineate it from any other object.
The question is, of course, why should the ID have anything to do with genius. The answer is simple and we have already described it.
All life strives to be the unique representation of God, as was mentioned.
Man is no exception.
The ID cannot actually think for itself but it does have awareness - the awareness that it is the basic form of man - so it also strives to be the one aspect of God, the life force.
Thus, in order to try to become this unique aspect of God, it puts ideas into the minds of certain people and they bring these ideas into the public's view and we say they are flashes of genius.
This is so that the ID feels that it is closer to grasping what God is.

It must be said that not everyone is capable of being used by the ID to have an original thought placed in them.

For many people it is not in their life plan to follow the difficult and lonely path that geniuses take.

However, it is said that everyone has their hour of glory and so everyone can be given an original thought. Whether they choose to develop that thought and bring it into the public domain is a different matter but, certainly, every one is given something of interest at least once in their lives.

And so the subject of imagination is complex and goes far beyond what most people think concerning it.

Indeed, imagination is a spiritual force that is closely connected to higher mind and, in many people, replaces higher mind which can be both positive and catastrophic depending on which action is taken to set the wheels of creation in motion as the person concerned allows his imagination to control his actions.

Thus we can see how important it is for people to learn to still their imagination and allow higher mind to pass uninterrupted through the layers of imagination and to go directly into mind, allowing mind to be controlled by higher self and not for mind to be under the control of imagination.

We turn now to another aspect of life known as determination.

This word, determination is greatly misunderstood. It usually is taken to imply 'pig headiness', 'one track mind' and so on.

In fact determination is quite important and without determination a person would be swept about by all the mass of information coming into his mind from a variety of sources.

With determination active and fully trained, it is possible to achieve great things.

If we look at many highly successful people, whatever field of activity they pursued, we can see a constant thread of a single activity they pursued from childhood until dotage.

This is determination at work, pushing a person to follow a single course of action throughout their life.

We must point out that determination should be used with circumspect as few people live solitary lives, cut off from any family, friends, business or social contracts.

Should a person pursue his chosen course without regard for the feelings and desires of others he would become the rather unpleasant person we sometimes see when observing a person totally encased in determination, following his chosen path regardless of others.
Thus, determination should be balanced with a large degree of self denial. Indeed, self denial could be considered to be the opposite of determination. Someone who embraces self denial pushes aside any desire to advance for himself and puts himself at the service of those more determined.

Thus it is noticeable that people who have determination developed and push forward a single agenda, often have one or more people that are at their beck and call doing whatever the determined person commands them to do, so that the person is totally free to concentrate on his project.
There are not only individuals totally engaged by their determination. Most businesses have one determined goal.
Governments are similarly enwrapped - although it must be pointed out that to follow any particular agenda is not the panacea of the problems facing a country and a population but just the desires of those in power at the moment.
Eventually, they will lose power and another group takes over with projects opposite to the first which they push forward with great determination only, in turn, to be rejected by the voters when it became obvious that they too were pursuing empty dreams.
In all cases, there is the determination of one or more people concentrating all their efforts on a single goal.

As no one is an island, these few determined people surround themselves with people willing to subjugate their desires to the wishes of these few.
In the case of a government, there would be the president pursuing his agenda, various like-minded ministers and then an army of secretaries, lawyers, chauffeurs down to the chefs and cleaning staff all beavering away to make sure that the desires of one determined person succeeds.

Can we find, in nature, a parallel of this type of pyramidal structure?
Well, we find it in ants and bees, the whole colony working day and night to ensure that the queen ant or bee has optimal conditions to do her job which is to produce offspring, which she does with total determination.

We have mentioned ants and bees before and implied that it is, perhaps, not the best way for humanity to advance and have suggested that it is similar to the Archon concept, which is to have a chosen few living in great luxury at the top and all the rest working as slaves to keep their chosen few in the style that they enjoy.

This system has, of course, been used throughout the world for long ages and was the basis of slavery and serfdom and carries on to this day in many domains.
So, we have at one end of the scale people in total self denial and, at the other end, people totally determined to follow a course of action, whatever the consequences.
We must also remind people that psychopaths can fall into this category also, desirous of achieving a goal at any cost to others or, indeed, to the planet.
But we have said that times are changing and the time of the Archons is coming to a close.
This will mean that these hierarchical structures will crumble.
But, obviously, this must be done slowly and carefully to avoid the chaos that would ensue if this system was disbanded overnight.

Now, how will this change of attitude affect those with determination highly developed and are convinced of the course of action they follow?
If we remember that this change is a spiritual one and that all humanity is actually one, over time, a spiritual change will come to determined people and, indeed to those in self denial, and that will result in those with determination highly developed to start to think about the needs and want of others.
Equally, those who have subjugated their will to the desires of the first group will find their self confidence growing and will, themselves, start to develop the desire to create.
This will result in a coming together, a joining of desires, not to push one selfish act forward, but the desire to act together for God and for man and create solutions to problems that will benefit all mankind.

Just to finish off this subject, should anyone question, it is not our intention to interfere with the ant or bee population. Man has already caused enough harm to the bee population.

These tiny creatures, ants and bees, have been created by God for a purpose and we have no desire to intervene in God's master plan.

The next subject to which we must turn our attention is that of motive. Why should motive come into the picture of the ascent of man towards God? Quite simply because we should analyze our motives for why we do anything. Everything is of importance in life from the smallest action taken to the master plan of God itself. God has a motive for doing what it does and, as we all have the God spirit within us, it follows that we, too, must have a motive for what we do.

The difference, of course, between us and God is that God concentrates all of his energy, if we can put it thus, in creating conditions where we, through our various experiences, help God to grow in wisdom, whereas we have many things that distract us and have more or less importance in our lives.

Some of the things that we decide to do seem to have little or no effect on the unveiling of our life plan, whereas other things that occupy our intentions have life changing effects.
But they all come from motive.
So motive is an important, if neglected, part of man's make-up.

Can we find out where this object we call motive resides in the hierarchy of the human spiritual construction?
There are some parts of humanity that we have not yet discussed and we do not wish to confuse you by mentioning aspects of life that we have not yet explained but we wish to give a brief overview of the construction of man from a spiritual point of view.
So we ignore the physical body for the moment and turn our attention to the spiritual aspects of man.
These are many and we have only mentioned a few.
We must also say that each aspect of humanity resides in one of the eight dimensions, although, as we have said they are not exactly spiritual planes, spiritual galaxies. They are levels of spirituality so the higher the spiritual level, the closer it becomes to God itself.

So let us now, briefly, examine these aspects of man and state where they are placed in relation to God at one end of the chain and nadir at the other.

God, as we know is actually above and beyond even, the highest plane, being the creator of them all.
We cannot create anything from the level of the plane where the creation is happening.
We must create from a higher level.
As we assume that God created all of the levels of man's growth so we must assume that we must be less than God.

And yet we have stated that we are God.
Once again we have this problem to resolve.
How can we be God and yet, if we were created by God and therefore must be lesser than God, be resolved?
The answer lies in the collective consciousness, the ID.

We have mentioned that we are all one and that one is God and we are part of and totality of God. This difficult to understand aspect can only be resolved when we can accept that the thing called collective consciousness, that we term the ID, is our connection to God.
Now, we prefer to use the term ID rather than collective consciousness because the latter can be manipulated by powerful minds, for better or for worse, but the ID remains steadfast. It is our connection to God.
Therefore, in the chain of spiritual progressions, we have the ID, of which there is just one for humans incarnate, discarnate and for those experiencing life in different dimensions.

Thus we start with the ID.
Below that, but closely connected to ID is higher self, also known as higher mind.
Higher mind is our personal aspect of ID, and thus our personal aspect of God.
Each higher self is unique and yet, together our higher minds can join in an effort to push life towards perfection.
Just below higher mind we find imagination.
As we have already explained, imagination can work with higher mind and that produces what we term genius, It also allows someone to become a great spiritual leader. Jesus and Buddha immediately spring to mind.

Below imagination in the chain of construction of man we find will, the desire to construct either mentally or physically.

Next comes determination. The drive to achieve a result, a goal.
Then we go onto the mind, which is the spiritual aspect of brain and lastly, in this brief and incomplete overview is the physical brain.

But we ignored motive. Why did we do this?
For the simple reason that motive is not actually part of the chain of spiritual constructs that we just mentioned.
All the above-mentioned aspects are firmly implanted in various dimensions, various auras but motive is not.
It is outside of those fixed attributes.
Motive exists but can jump about somewhat and can influence the person at different levels of intention.
Motive can influence the higher mind to do wonderful, holy things or it can push someone at the lowest aura, to cause terrible harm.
And yet it exists and one would reasonably expect it to have a home base in one of the planes of spirituality.
But it does not. It flitters about from level to level always trying to influence a person that it is doing something correct.
It can be controlled, and should be, yet for many people it is motive that justifies their actions for good or for bad.
Motive is the force that tries to persuade people to take action in whatever direction the person wishes to go.

Thus we have tried to impress upon you all that the invisible, spiritual aspects of man's creation are real and indeed, more real than the physical body and will out last the physical body for a long time because the spiritual aspect, being connected to God itself is, thus, immortal, or virtually so. It only disappears from view the moment that it rejoins God itself and that is a long way into the future for all of us.

And yet, there is a vast amount of energy spent by all professionals of medicine, clothes and furniture manufactures, housing and vehicle construction all of which is designed to assist the physical body - and quite rightly so because man has the right to live in comfort - but there is actually very little effort made to help man understand and comprehend the importance of his spiritual bodies.

The reason behind this has already been discussed at some length.

We spoke about the Archons who were permitted to influence man during the time that the pendulum of life was in the negative part returning energy back to God.
We also mentioned that most religions and schools were created by and under the control of psychopathic people, themselves under the control of the Archons.

Now, we break off once again to assure the reader that when we consider the Archon and Archon controlled people enslaving the minds and, sometimes, the bodies of humanity, we are in no way criticizing them.
We use the term psychopath in its medical sense not in the understanding that has grown up today with all its evil connotations.

All this dark stuff that went on for so long was an essential part of God's plan to return energy to God to recharge the batteries of life, and so, had to be.
The evil, that we would all like to have reduced if we could have, was an essential part of life.
We could not have the sweet without, first, tasting the bitter.

So, man has been educated that all that exists is physical matter and anything spiritual is just the ravings of lunatic people who were regularly locked up or killed if they dared talk about spirituality.
When we use the word spirituality we are not including religion.
Religion is an Archon invention and therefore was an unfortunate but necessary part of darkness.

The life of Jesus is given to us to show us how the negative priests of Israel could not accept the light from the teachings of Jesus to shine into their dark world, frightening them as they saw truth for an instance and so they did all that was in their power to shut off that light until, much later, other minds could invent a form of interpretation of the wisdom of Jesus that would please the Archon masters still hiding in the dark.

Fear was and is behind any negative action, so fear has been created for all that time to allow the Archons to live in shadow.
Truth creates light and light chases darkness.

We have mentioned that all life everywhere in our galaxy is now moving into the light, God's light, and is starting to chase darkness.

We do not wish to labor the point but we do wish to say this:
It is time for man to start to move his attention away from physical things and start to concentrate more on spiritual things.
There is nothing wrong with outdoor exercise, healthy food and happiness but there is a lot wrong with allowing sports - which are a relic of the gladiator days - to occupy such an important place in people's lives.
There is a lot wrong with using drugs and strong drinks and even tobacco unless used in a medicinal sense.
There is a lot wrong with such concentrated thought on material wealth and objects.
Similarly, there is a lot wrong with allowing politicians who cannot know how to run a country, to do so, because they do not have access to higher self which is the seat of wisdom.
The way education is conducted is nothing short of criminal in many countries.
All this exists because of the concentration of the minds of people on physicality at the expense of spirituality.
All this was inevitable during the pendulum swing in darkness.

Now, however, we are moving into the light and man must shift his attention away from physicality and materialism and start to inhabit his spiritual bodies. It is time for man to pack his bags and move from his house of darkness into his house of light which is awaiting him, the door wide open and light flooding out to welcome him.

In the next chapter we will discuss how to make this move and what the results should be.

CHAPTER SEVEN

INTO THE KNOWN

The pendulum swing that we have previously mentioned, moving from spiritual darkness into the glory of spiritual light has, of course, been going on for eons of time both emptying and recharging God's batteries, if we may use that analogy, implying that even God does not have unlimited energy and that, at a certain point in the emptying of God's battery, it runs out of power and thus, has to be recharged again thanks to the negativity created by moving into spiritual darkness.

It is hoped that the student can appreciate by now that we are just using mental images when we talk about God having batteries, but the concept of electricity, using and replacing it, is close enough to reality to serve our purpose.

There is no point in using complex imagery nor employing complex terms to describe God in action when there are simple examples, with which all are familiar, to describe reality at work.

So, as we have said, God's batteries are now fully charged and this energy, being alive and being life itself, is acting like a foetus of a person or an animal awaiting the wonderful moment when it can extricate itself from its mother's womb and appear in the light of day.

Once again this is an analogy, and not a very good one, but how can one describe the power of God making itself manifest especially as, this light, although invisible to most people, being pure spirituality, nevertheless is the basis of all life.

Therefore, we have this ineluctable progression from darkness to light, from fear of the unknown into positivity, love and self assuredness.

Now, we mentioned in the title of this chapter that life is moving from the unknown into the known and yet, for most of us, both incarnate and discarnate, all any of us have known is the negative period that has occupied all of our minds for, virtually as long as we can remember.

As we who are discarnate, even the more recent arrivals, communicate with discarnate beings that have been in the spiritual realms for a long time, their memories are filled with times, with long centuries, of war and bloodshed!

There were very few moments of light during those dark ages and they were, indeed dark and dismal times.

However, man is not limited to just that period of time.

The life span of a human is virtually infinite going in both directions from the present.

This implies that all life existed long before any concept of incarnation in physical form was conceived.

In the case of humans, the logos of what we term a human existed in the high astral realms long before it was called forth to assume its role as a recognisable form of human.

We wish to discuss just what this logos, this embryo human was and where it was located in the spiritual planes.

We have previously mentioned that all is one and that one is God.

We have also mentioned that this oneness can assume an almost infinite variety of forms; animal, vegetable and mineral.

We mentioned the ID, and said that it was the basic logos of humanity, the archetypal concept of a human.

So can we discover a bit more about this concept, why it exists and where it exists?

Thanks to the contribution made to this book by extremely advanced beings, themselves so advanced spiritually compared to most of us that they are barely visible to us, being just entities of pure spiritual light - the light of God - we have been able to piece together information concerning the actions taken by God in his quest for knowledge and wisdom.

We wish to underline our eternal thanks to these beings who descended to our level in order to answer our questions and to share their knowledge with us, without which much of this book would not have been written.

We are happy to share this knowledge with you and hope that you, too, can appreciate with gratitude the guidance obtained.

So, it appears that the God-force, on the eighth plane, was able to create astral forms to explore that plane and experience the life that God created.

As was mentioned, this was a long time ago, indeed, so we can say, ignoring any and all other forms of life created at that time, and concentrating exclusively on humanity, that man has, to all intents and purpose, always existed although, as has already been mentioned, the human forms that inhabited and explored the eighth plane, or carrier wave, bore little resemblance to man as he appears today.

He was purely an astral entity which implies that he was of light.

This light form still exists associated with humanity and, when we can shake off the illusional form created by ego, man will, once again, assume his body of light.

Thus we can state that this astral form (astral both in its connotation of dimensions and in its starlight meaning) is the basic logos of man and this man, when he is ready will be able to return to this known form that has always been associated with him.

Let us move down from the eighth plane, which we have already described in some detail in an earlier chapter, to an area where events that are more easily comprehensible occur.

Now, to repeat what we have already said, man, in his, primal form is pure light, without form although we will say that the logos of humanity is spherical, a ball of light.

This light contains all the elements that go to make a man with the exception of ego.

Thus we find higher self, determination, will, imagination and emotion amongst other attributes with the exception of ego, which does not appear until much later in the life of a person.

This light form is the concept that humanity will eventually reassume when ego diminishes enough to allow the light of God to shine forth from him.

This is the point that we need to break off from describing the basic logos of man to elucidate how we create our human shape that we all have or have had at some point in our existence.

It must at all times be remembered that we are one with God and thus we are one logos or ID.

But it is that ID that enables us to assume a unique identity.

This is where we have to bring into the picture something that is called the 'oversoul'.

Oversoul is that which acts like a parent to us.

When we start to assume a more recognisable form than just pure light, we are put in the care of something that is termed the oversoul.

Actually, the oversoul is a construct that has been created by angelic forces to act rather like parents do, guiding us and nurturing our existence in whatever plane of reality we move to.

The oversoul is not a person as we would know a parent but it exists and acts as a sort of home base for us, our home while we need one.

Once again, the oversoul is nonphysical and does not really exist except as a concept, a place that we can call home.

Thus it is very precious and all humans accept that they belong to an oversoul.

It gives a feeling of security to know that we have a home, a place in which we are cared for and loved rather as a child, providing that he lives in a good home, returns to with pleasure at the end of each day away from home.

It is from the oversoul that we get the concept, on Earth, of forming families.

Now, the oversoul does not create life. All life was created by God long ago and waits in the highest realm as an astral form, pure light, until it is time for it to enter the stage of active life.

It is at this point that the embryo life form, life spirit, is put into the care of an oversoul.

We break off at this point to indicate that oversouls act in a sort of pyramidal concept.

At the lowest point they are numerous but, oversouls exist in higher forms, stacked on top of each other in decreasing numbers until, finally, there is only one and that one is God.

Anyway, we return to our embryo human spirit which is put, by angels, into the care of an oversoul at the lowest level but which is, nevertheless, from a spiritual point of view, far in advance than anything that we could imagine.

At this point, the embryo spirit could be considered very much to be like a newborn babe, totally dependant on the oversoul to care for it.

Therefore, it is nurtured over a long period of time by both angelic beings and others who dedicate their existence to the correct upbringing of embryo humanity.

Just as Earthly parents nurture their children, so these beings, some of whom are advanced humans and some, angelic beings who are of a difference life plan, look after these young human spirits.

The object is to bring into the awareness of these young spirits the various concepts that will enable them to realize what it means to be a human, because, although the embryo spirits have the human logos associated with them as opposed to animal or any other life form, the spirit itself, at the beginning of its long journey through human existence has no concept of what being a human entails.

Thus a long period of patient education ensues, gradually bringing into this young spirit's awareness that it is a human and what all that entails.

In this way, the spirit, which is still very much connected to its home base, the oversoul, gradually develops, mentally, emotionally and spiritually, as much information as it feels capable of absorbing.

It should be pointed out that, just as all people are different, so all spirits are different and some advance more easily in any one direction than others.

As there are an almost infinite number of things to learn and an almost infinite number of directions a spirit can be drawn towards, it takes very clever and devoted educators to help the spirit control his chosen direction.

Then, as was described in the previous volume in this series (The Stairway To Freedom), the spirit that wishes to have a physical incarnation gradually works his way towards Earth, eventually to be born in his chosen sex and family to start his long journey back again to the point he started.

The difference, of course, the whole purpose of the voyage, being to grow in wisdom through an almost infinite number of experiences and all that knowledge and wisdom is fed, via a series of oversouls, back into the Godhead and God, too, grows in wisdom.

It should be realized that during these various incarnations, first on Earth, and then on other planes of spirituality, known as dimensions, the oversoul is always monitoring the progress of his charge, the human spirit. It does not, generally speaking, interfere with the progress of that spirit but it can should it feel that things are going seriously astray.

However, like most good parents it allows its young charge to experiment for itself, to try its strength and to grow through the experiences that it draws towards itself.

We break off in our discussion of the oversoul to return to the word 'incarnations' that we mentioned.

We have already explained that, for the vast majority of humanity, they have just one incarnation in physicality on planet Earth.

For a long time the concepts of multiple incarnations in human form has been put into the minds of generations.

This concept is, of course, once again, an Archon one.

The Archons being almost AI (artificial intelligence) in nature have great difficulty in inventing original thought and so they usually take an existing fact, turn it on its head and present it as a negative concept in order to create fear.

Incarnations is just one more such way the Archons work.

Certainly, there are a number of incarnations, if one can describe the progress through life of a person but, we repeat, generally speaking, almost without exception, a human - or animal for that matter - has just one incarnation in physicality.

All other incarnations occur in the astral realms of spiritual progression and are not so much incarnations as progressions from one plane of spirituality to another.

We hope that, as we progress further into the light shining on us from the source of all life - God -, so this false concept will come to be seen for what it is, an Archon invention.

We further realize that it will take a lot of mental effort by some people who have, not only the concept of multiple incarnations firmly engrained in their minds, but have built a whole story, a whole concept of how life is constructed around this false concept.

There are some people who write books and give lectures expounding this incorrect idea and we are sorry to say that their egos will take a blow when they will have to admit that the concept of reincarnation and much other related information that they have been expounding to a gullible public was false.

One can easily imagine that, even when they realize the truth, having to face the public and admit their error would be devastating to their status as gurus of spiritual wisdom and so, we expect, that many will cling to and expound this false idea for a long while into the future, hoping that the public who follow their teachings will never find the truth for themselves.

Of course, the truth will out one day and the inevitable blow to egos will occur.

However, truth is better than fiction and those who have embraced lies should have taken the trouble to seek the truth before putting pen to paper and just following conventional wisdom instead of doing original research on the subject.

To return to the oversoul.

As was mentioned, the oversoul which, we explain again, is not a person but a concept, a consciousness, nevertheless has intelligence.

All is one. Therefore all the attributes that humans have, oversouls also have.

Thus, we can compare an oversoul to a loving parent always keeping a parental eye on its offspring.

It must be said that most people incarnate have never heard about oversouls and thus have no idea that there is always a strong bond between themselves and their oversoul.

This is unfortunate and will change.

Once again it is to the Archons that we must attribute this secrecy concerning one's oversoul.

In order to hide the spiritual aspect of humanity from people, naturally it was in their interests to keep knowledge about this parental guidance from the public.

This will obviously change as we move into the bright future and people will learn to contact their oversoul for guidance.

The oversoul is not higher self. As was mentioned, it is a concept rather as we have the concept of 'home'. A safe haven to return to when it is necessary.

Thus the oversoul is a very important element in the makeup of humanity.

It is the oversoul's duty, in conjunction with various angelic beings, to prepare the 'student' human for his long voyage into the unknown we call life.

Now, we should say that not all young humans have Earthly incarnations.

The baby human, as soon as he is ready to make decisions concerning his future, feels drawn, by the law of mutual attraction, towards a certain area of life.

This may be an Earthly incarnation or it may be to stay in the higher astral spheres and advance in that way.

Or again, it may go off to one of the astral areas surrounding a planet somewhere and become what Earth people call an alien.

We should say that some young humans are drawn towards the dark side of life and will descend to the lower regions, not necessarily in an evil sense as imagined by man, but in order to work with the negative spirits whose job it is to help keep the planet Earth in balance from a point of view of growth and decline.

It is imagined by many that if there was only positive growth, life would be paradisiacal, but, in fact it would cause chaos.

We need balance between growth and decline for order to be maintained and so these brave souls volunteer to descend to those dark areas to assist the angels of destruction in their duties.

This, as one can imagine, is a very unpleasant but necessary task and it takes a very special, courageous person to spend long ages working in abysmal conditions to aid and control the actual negative angels tasked with destruction.

Equally, other humans might be drawn to assist the angels of growth, if we may call them this, which is a hard but more pleasant job.

So the student of esoteric matters can see that there are a large number of areas that a young human might be drawn to, only one of which involves an Earthly incarnation.

But our field of concentration at the moment centers on those that decide to descend to Earth.

We described, both in this book and, more extensively in the first volume (The Stairway To Freedom) that not all young humans have exactly the same views on God, spirituality and the makeup of life.

Just as people on Earth find mathematics or foreign languages easy or difficult to assimilate, so young spirits in the care of an oversoul find themselves more or less attracted to the spiritual concepts.

Once the oversoul, in conjunction with angelic help, locate a person who cannot accept the education given to him concerning God etc, no one tries to force him but he will be offered the opportunity of going to Earth, which is the plane of existence where the people of Earth have either a twisted view of spirituality or reject the notion of God altogether.

This, as we now know is the result of Archon intervention - a sad but necessary event in the pendulum swing of life.

And so, for long ages, a certain section of young humanity was attracted to Earth.

We break off once again to say that the afore mentioned pendulum swing has been, for some time, moving into the light areas and that light has been shining in the higher astral planes for quite a long while, illuminating every aspect of the higher planes and thus, as a consequence, it has become normal for more and more young spirits to become spiritually awake.

This has resulted in a lesser number of young humans coming to Earth in total denial of God and more volunteering to come to Earth to assist with the awakening process for those already incarnate who have, themselves, their spiritual awareness firmly in place.

Now, this change in optic has only just started. As we progress more and more into the light, so we will have a decrease in the numbers of young people who leave their oversoul in denial of God and more who will choose to incarnate on Earth fully equipped to help push all humanity incarnate forward more quickly.

It has to be said that the evil ones, under the control of the Archons, are also fully aware of this change and are doing all that they can to limit the effectiveness of these young souls using injections and drugs of various kinds to damage the fragile physical bodies of these brave young souls.

The body may be damaged and communication between the spiritual aspects and the physical aspects impaired, but the evil ones cannot damage the spiritual aspects.

Unfortunately, the only way these young humans have of transmitting their wisdom is through telepathy.

As very few people incarnate have bothered to learn telepathy, these wise beings are trapped within their damaged bodies and are unable to fulfil the function that they incarnated to do.

It is hoped that, soon, a solution to this problem will be found and the world will be flooded with spiritual wisdom but, first, the power of the evil ones will need to be diminished, which brings us back again to the spiritual change that will assist in the removal from influence of evil people still firmly in place in so many domains.

Let us now assume that a young human, whatever his level of spiritual awareness, has now left the safety of his oversoul and has taken the plunge towards Earth.

We have already described the different, descending planes of existence that the person, in astral form, descends to in a previous tome (The Stairway To Freedom), so we will not repeat it here except to say that the person gradually descends to the point where he can be born on Earth into his chosen family and future.

The student of the mysteries of life will need first to read and comprehend the information contained in the first volume of The Stairway To Freedom or much of what we talk about will not be understood.

So, we will assume that a baby is born and gradually grows to become a young adult.

We will stop this chapter here, which dealt mainly with the 'birth' in the spiritual realms of an embryo spirit and its growth in the care of its oversoul, to the point that it was ready to take its next step into life.

In the next chapter we will attempt to describe what an incarnation is and its purpose so that the student can better comprehend the way his life is unfolding.

CHAPTER EIGHT

THE HARD LIFE

This chapter, which will describe an Earthly incarnation, with all its trials and tribulations is, in a way, a continuation of the previous one, as the descent into physicality and the experiences, whilst in physicality, are part of the same long process from leaving the safety of the oversoul to the moment of release from physicality and the return home.

So, we part here from the moment when a baby is born and the spirit, which is the true person, associates itself with that baby, that human foetus and the baby springs to life. We say that a baby is born and the parents, generally, rejoice.

It must be said that, for long ages while the pendulum swing was in the negative part of God's kingdom, those who had nurtured that astral spirit for so long were sad, knowing the suffering that their charge would go through as he progressed through life until the moment of his release and return to the heavenly spheres.

So we have the parents of a newborn babe rejoicing but we have its spiritual parents sad. At the end of life, we have people, generally, sad at the demise of a loved one, whilst the angels rejoice at the safe return of their charge, battered and bruised by his incarnation but nevertheless, safe and sound and welcomed back, once again, into the familiarity of his oversoul, and all the friends and family that may also belong to that oversoul.

Then the angels, who have closely watched over the spirit during its Earthly incarnation, sing for joy at the safe return home of their charge.

Events that can occur when a person returns home will be discussed in a later chapter but, for the moment, we are concerned with the Earthly incarnation, its purpose and its objective.

So, we have a newborn babe, born into its chosen family, with its chosen sex orientation, born into the country of its choice, the language of that country and the family's social standing, rich or poor, highly educated or ignorant of such knowledge.

All this was carefully chosen by the spirit in conjunction with guides and angels long before the baby was thought of, when it was just a twinkle in the parent's eye, as the saying goes because it is at this point that decisions are beings taken by the angels as to who will be incarnate in that family.

And so we have a baby that is going to be lovingly nurtured, one hopes, by its parents.

This is not always the case, of course, but this would already have been known to the incarnating spirit who purposely chose to be born to gain experience - unpleasant as it will be - to further the knowledge fed, via his oversoul, into the God-force. All knowledge is precious, not just pleasant knowledge but unpleasant as well.

Now, we break off completely in our description of incarnation, which, incidentally means 'in the flesh', to question why a human is born with the form that he has.

After all, the incarnating spirit is pure light so it might seem logical that the human form would follow that shape and a baby born as a round ball, a sphere, like its incarnating spirit.

It will be quickly realized that such a shape would be ridiculous. A ball might be the correct shape for people to kick around a field but would not be very practical for developing life on Earth.

Those who examine life on Earth have realized that most creatures follow a basic pattern, which is a head, a body, two arms and two legs.

This form was chosen by the archangelic beings who were tasked with creating life forms in physicality because it obviously gave the greatest chance of mobility and the ability to feed and defend itself.

Virtually all creatures have this basic form although some have alerted their shape in order either to develop different methods of locomotion or to live in different environments.

We are thinking, for example of birds who have altered their arms to make wings in order to fly.

Also fish spring to mind, as well as dolphins and whales, who have, once again sacrificed arms and legs in order to be able to swim in water.

We could go on but we wish to make quite clear to you that this basic shape that we described was chosen because it enabled life to develop more quickly.

It will be noted that creatures that chose not to develop arms and legs; snails, clams and various other life forms have not really developed at all for millions of years because life without true mobility and arms to gather food or to defend oneself have caused a barrier to progression.

We wish the readers of this book also to accept that when alien life creates robotic life forms to visit Earth, almost invariably they choose some form of this basic pattern previously described as they have noticed that it gives their created life forms the greatest chance to operate on Earth and occasionally to pass unnoticed by real humans on Earth.
Some of these created life forms, which, we repeat are actually robots, resemble humanity so much that they can move amongst us undetected.
It would only be a person with psychic abilities highly developed that could detect that these entities are not real humans but soulless robotic life forms.

However, we return to the born babe who, we hope, has a body exactly like his parents in miniature.
We feel the desire to sympathize with the suffering that the mother went through to deliver the baby and that is because the human abdomen is poorly developed for producing offspring compared to animals - who, incidentally, were developed to populate planet Earth - humans being more recent visitors. The body of a human female would have to be greatly modified in order to give birth easily and we hardly think that the resulting body shape would be considered attractive to modern females.
So, the struggle to help a baby be born continues.
The aforementioned baby is completely helpless for several months, until it develops the power to stand up and walk.
So it, in its early stages, depends on adults to feed, clothe and generally care for the young person.

Once again we break off to compare a baby in its prime infancy to many animals who, just minutes after being born, can stand, walk and even run - something that a human baby cannot do for a long time.
This indicates to us quite clearly that we humans are not natural to planet Earth but are visitors that incarnate for a purpose which will be explained later.
So we watch the baby grow, take its first steps and starts to become a real thinking human, getting more and more independent from its parents, although in most good families, the parents keep a close eye on their charge to protect it from making drastic errors from a physical or mental point of view.
As so the infant grows.

Generally speaking he concentrates all his energies on exploring the world around him and is totally ignorant of any spiritual aspect to him, despite him being made totally from God-force.

We fast forward a few years to the point where the child is able to think for itself.
Now, if the educational system was better structured, the spiritual aspect of humanity would be very much included in the educational curriculum but, generally speaking it isn't.
In many schools today, any mention of spirituality is banned. Even in so called religious schools, spiritual education is limited to learning lessons from books about religion and so the child will leave that school with little or no knowledge of the nature of spirituality.
This, of course, as has been already mentioned, is the work of the Archons and their minions who run educational systems in much of the world.
It is hoped that this will change as and when the Archons and the psychopaths are removed from any sphere of influence.
But at the moment we must accept life as it is with all it faults and it is our task to produce information that will provide some level of education to seekers after truth.

So the child grows, following a curriculum of education strictly controlled by evil forces that ensure that when that child leaves school he might have some degree, if extremely limited, of knowledge of basic education but that curriculum has totally ignored any mention of spirituality as opposed to religion.
It will be noticed by older generations that even the knowledge imparted concerning basic skill patterns - reading, writing, maths, geography and so on is extremely limited compared with education implanted in the minds of the young years ago and so many leave school with no real ability to communicate by the written or spoken word, no ability - or very little - to calculate and virtually no knowledge of geography of the world.
The excuse given is that, in a modern world where computer devices can do so much for us, there is no need to learn basic skills.
A moments thought should indicate that this is a blatant attempt by the evil ones to stifle the brain's ability to think because the brain is a tool that can expand or contract, not physically, but intellectually, according to how much use one makes of it.

One can compare the brain to a muscle which, through exercise can grow stronger and can serve the body more effectively whereas, if use is not made of those same muscles, they atrophy and are unable to be used by the person in an effective manner.
The brain is much the same.
Intellectual stimulus causes it to grow stronger and lack of stimulus causes it to diminish.
Learning to operate a computer is an important part of modern life but in no way can it replace studying and manipulating language or mathematics.
One wonders if the day will ever come when there will be no one left to create the language or mathematical programs.
Then, if that sad day should ever occur, there would be nothing left to appear on the computer screen.

We should perhaps reveal that this scenario has already been considered by the evil ones and they are developing Artificial Intelligence to take over when and if the human brain should stop.
However, we fully expect this unhappy event will never be brought to fruition because of the timely move of the galaxy into the light of God which will chase the evil ones and their horrible plans from ever becoming reality.
We expect that the more traditional forms of education will return and we will have a happy blend of fully active brains working alongside AI, the computers reducing the chores of communication and calculation but, never the less, children being taught to think and communicate fully as was intended by God when he created life.
In the meantime, all over the world we have generations of people unable to think for themselves and are thus easy to manipulate by the evil ones.

Let us know move onto the moment when the young person leaves school but, instead of being armed to assume his place and his role in adult environment, is really only able to do manual labor or join the countless unemployed masses.
All this was planned long ago.
We have intelligent young men and women totally incapable of assuming any real role in society and forced to accept low paid employment, if they can find a place, or forced to spend long years barely surviving on unemployment handouts.

Unemployment is not a natural way for humans to live.
We should all be in a position to contribute to society instead of taking from it.
Also, there is an old but true expression, 'the devil finds work for idle hands'.
This, once again is the plan of the evil ones who provide drugs in unlimited quantities to further cause atrophy of what little brain is left for many.
Then the entertainment media provide endless violence in the form of news and films, once again, carefully planned so that people grow considering that violence is a normal part of life.
So people pass their time in a confused state, unable to understand why they are here on Earth and what purpose life holds.

This lack of information concerning the function of humanity and its relation to God and to all of God's creation is, as has been already explained, deliberately planned and carefully put into operation.
If people are kept in the dark concerning their origins and their destiny while, at the same time leaving them without any real means of thinking for themselves nor any effective ability to read and write, the effect of all that is generations stumbling through life in a depressed, confused and bitter state of mind, which is the complete opposite of the way that life was meant to develop.
Imagine if it were possible for young people to be taught to think for themselves, to contact their higher selves, the source of all knowledge, to be able to share that knowledge via the spoken or written word and by telepathic communication, what a different world would be created.

It has previously been mentioned that the Archons, this race of etheric entities that have, unfortunately, been so necessary in the process of recharging God's batteries, cannot really think for themselves but are determined to destroy God's master plan for humanity as far as they can.
They are experts at taking anything good and positive, turning it upside down and presenting it as evil, influencing psychopathic controllers of humanity to enforce laws to forbid positive concepts and promoting negative concepts as the only way that humanity is allowed to act.
Thus we have the situation that exists today and that is hoped by the Archons and evil ones will continue for all eternity.

As we have explained, their plan will fail but, for the mean time it is in full swing and we must live in this reality until we can bring about change as we move gradually into the light.

Let us continue with the story of young people growing to maturity, thinking that this sad world in with they live is normal and is the only way life can be. Now, at school today, sex education, which has long been a bone of contention by prudish educationalists in the past must be discussed.
Until fairly recently, it was generally ignored in schools, and young people grew to manhood (or womanhood) with their only knowledge about the opposite sex being gleaned from photographs purchased under the counter from purveyors of semi-pornographic material!
Any discussion of the physical attributes of the opposite sex was discouraged and thus some people were greatly surprised when they did discover just what the opposite sex actually looked like.
There are stories, treated in comical fashion, of people getting married in total ignorance of the difference between men and women and how the procreation act is performed and were horrified when they discovered the truth on their wedding night.
This situation was, of course, ridiculous.
One of the reasons that man incarnates is to provide others to incarnate and the sex act is the prime method of doing this.
This is the reason that the sex drive is so powerful in young people.

Once again we see in religions how something perfectly normal and necessary to the continuance of humanity was banned until the 'sacred' day of marriage and then the couple, safely enmeshed in whatever religion that they were involved in, were encouraged to produced as many offspring as possible, all the children being captured into the same religion, thus allowing this religion to have a greater stranglehold on the world's population.
In some countries today, it is law that all people of those countries must be part of that religion and the religion and the law of the country being one and the same.
This was largely the case throughout the world until fairly recent times until a split between church and state was introduced, not in an attempt by the state to free the people from the clutches of the church, but so that the state could assume the role of guardians of the people.

It was and is just another means of controlling humanity under the pretext of liberating them.
So, once again, we were in a situation where the young were kept in the dark about such a simple and necessary process - the sex act.
Eventually, in some countries it was decided that sex education should be introduced.

One would think this would be a good and positive move towards decomplexing young people about the mysteries of the opposite sex.
However, we must always remember that the Archons are never far away, active and ready to seize on any positive idea, turn it on its head and create evil from it if they can.
Thus, as how to present sex education to young people was being considered, the concept of homosexuality was brought up and much thought, by those under the control of the Archons, was given into how to twist it into something evil.
So, the inevitable idea that homosexuality is a good and natural act - the opposite of how nature would naturally manifest itself - was brought into the educational system and introduced.
Now, naturally, we must explain and qualify that statement.

This has already been discussed at length in the book, The Stairway To Freedom, and we encourage all who are in confusion concerning homosexuality to peruse that book for a full explanation.

However, for those who have not read that book we will state that it occurs, from time to time, a person who incarnates in a body whilst his spirit, his personality is of the opposite sex to the body in which he incarnates.
This happens and, although it is the opposite to what should occur, we accept that a homosexual is born and must follow his instincts. We do not condemn that because it is very courageous of the individual to accept to incarnate in a body with which he is not, emotionally in agreement.

But, as we just mentioned, the Archon controlled people in charge of education systems seized upon the concept as a means of sowing yet more discord, which is always their aim.
So, teachers were instructed to educated young, confused children to experiment with same gender sex.

This obviously is evil and will be abolished as soon as the power of the evil ones is reduced.
Luckily, the majority of those children reject this evil and turn towards relationships with members of the opposite sex.
Thus, a degree of balance is restored.

Eventually, the young people turn to the idea of forming a permanent relationship with someone of the opposite sex.
Once again, this has been discussed at length in the first volume of this series of books and we don't wish to bore you by repeating endlessly information that, if you had read the first volume as we suggested, you should already be familiar.
So the young people reach out and, by the law of mutual attraction, manage to find a partner.
This concept of living in a relationship with another person is actually a lot more complicated than appears on the surface.
The relationship functions on many levels and should not be entered into lightly.
Unfortunately, for various reasons, the bond is usually sealed through the sex act. Once this occurs, it is a tacit agreement that a partnership is bonded.
This is unfortunate because, all too often, once the first excitement caused by the sex act passes, the couple find that they do not actually have very much in common and so the partnership fails.
It would be far better if the people took the time really to get to know each other before sealing the bond through the sex act instead of, as is so often the case, the sex part passes first and the 'getting to know each other' part passes last.
The result is the endless stream of broken relationships, unwanted children and general unhappiness instead of loving family relationships that should occur.
Do we, once again, feel the hand of the Archons promoting this upside down way of living?

So we suggest a more sensible way of forming families, one where young people meet a number of potential partners, get to know them well and await the gestalt moment that will eventually occur when the chosen partner comes into view.

Everyone has at least one perfect partner, there may be more than one, but there is at least one partner for each person with whom the individual under discussion can share his incarnation and with whom he can share the long ages in the spirit world when both incarnations have terminated.
Then will love last throughout the lives of the couple and then will children be raised in a loving relationship and broken marriages, with all the stress, trauma and unhappiness that the ending of a relationship entails, becomes a thing of the past instead of practically the norm as it is at the moment.
The Archons gain great power through the unhappiness caused by having chosen the wrong partner and we should all do what we can to lessen their stranglehold on us instead of feeding them as is the case now.

The technique for drawing the perfect partner has already been described elsewhere but it is important enough to repeat.
It, like all spiritual matters, is simple.
One sits on one's own in a room with any doors and windows shut, one quite simply asks God to send the perfect partner and then one thanks God that the message is being sent on the wings of angels to the person. Then, also, by the law of mutual attraction, those two people will eventually meet.
Patience and discernment will be required as the perfect partner may live far away but, rest assured that the couple will meet. Both will feel the gestalt formed when that magic event occurs. This gestalt is the result of the birth of love. Not passion, not desire but love.
This feeling of love will instantly fill the hearts of both people and will create a feeling of joy. This gestalt is unmistakable and all people desiring to meet their perfect partner should wait, with faith and expectancy, that glorious moment.

However, we must face reality as it exists for many couples who made hurried and incorrect marriages.
Once again, this subject has been discussed at length in the book 'Stairway To Freedom' and will not be discussed here except to say that, particularly when there are children involved, that it would be wise to repress ones disappointment in wrong decisions and try to live in harmony together.
The perfect partner can still be found by those in the heavenly spheres and then the couple can progress together throughout time in love.
An Earthly incarnation seems long but, out of all eternity it is not very long.

Most people find that their incarnation on Earth is hard.
Life is meant to be a joyous thing but how many people reach the end of it and look back with contentment, the joy of having passed a moment of their long existence as God itself in the bliss that we imagine that being God would entail?
Very few, we would suggest.
The vast majority of people, when their incarnation ends, and they find themselves in the love of the heavenly spheres, look back over their Earthly incarnation more as a nightmare incident and are only too glad that reincarnation is not a fact.
Very few people, indeed, would wish to return to this dark planet.
And yet, if we are all God, why is it that we have not collectively created paradise on Earth instead of this hellish place that we are only too glad to quit?

This, of course, has been explained in previous chapters where we elucidated the pendulum swing into and out of spiritual darkness.
So, there is little point in trying to explain the various traumas that an Earthly incarnation brings to us.
You who are incarnate at the moment, are only too aware of how disagreeable life on Earth is.
We mentioned it in order to assure you that this type of life will gradually draw to a close as the pendulum swings back again into spiritual light.
We must expect that the Archons and their psychopathic minions will do all that they can to stop this swing into spiritual light but, of course, they cannot. Nothing can halt this procession back and forth.
So, although we do fully appreciate that life for so many is scarcely bearable, but we ask you to be courageous and be assured that life will improve.

We, who dictate this book, also had Earthly incarnations, some of us at a time when things were a lot worse than they generally are now and some of us still bare the scars of that incarnation so we appreciate what you are going through.
But times change gradually and the time of evil is over.
Light, spiritual light is starting to pour into the auras of planet Earth and of all creatures and beings incarnate and will gradually eradicate the darkness.
Joy, love and harmony is the destiny of future man waiting to incarnate and they will lead a truly God filled life.

Please remember that God is everywhere and in all things but, as we mentioned, even God has to recharge his batteries, so to speak, in order to be able to illuminate future incarnations.

CHAPTER NINE

THE DYING PROCESS

Let us assume that all the readers of this book will be aware of the various types of employment taken by people, the different personalities that people have and the way that they pass their incarnation and fast forward to the point where the incarnation ends.

Once again, we will assume that some people pass naturally at the end of a long life while others find their term on Earth truncated by illness, accident, suicide and so forth.

No matter what the cause and what the duration of that life, in one way or another, most people will go to what are termed the heavenly spheres although, as we have mentioned in various talks, there are no domains but only levels of consciousness.

However, to avoid confusion, we will refer to heaven as a domain, a vast and many layered area that all souls go to at the end of their incarnation on Earth.

Before proceeding with details of how the transition from one plane to another occurs we should point out that planet Earth and all the so called physical galaxy fits into the description concerning the fact that it all only exists as a figment of our imagination.

All that may be observed is not real as people imagine it to be and exists by what is referred to as collective consciousness otherwise known as cosmic consciousness, the ID.

A better term would be cosmic illusion, but, as people reading this book can attest to, it appears real and solid.

In a similar fashion, the various levels of heaven appear just as real as the world in which you currently live in does.

Illusion can be very persuasive. Just as the vast majority of people incarnate are convinced that the Earth is a solid body and that all life that one can observe has physicality so the heavenly spheres appear as solid and real.

Indeed, few are the numbers of people able to see through the illusions either of physicality or of the higher levels that are referred to in many works on esoterics.

So long as things appear real there is no reason to question them.

So, as we mentioned, to avoid confusion, we also will follow the trend, consider Earth as solid and heaven as a plane, a dimension to where one migrates at the end of incarnation.

Now, we need to understand that a physical entity: man, animal or plant, has a physical body, the part that we are used to seeing because it is created from certain atoms that physicality requires and forms a shape according to the Logos of the creature,
We are all familiar with the shape that humans have, many animals and some plants.
Those shapes are created around the blueprint, the Logos of that entity.

However, the Logos is not a physical force, it is an invisible spiritual force and yet it can influence so called reality to create that which is observed by people and animals - physicality.

This physicality, so real, is almost an impossible concept to deny. What we see, what we feel, what we experience cannot be an illusion even if people like us who live in another dimension say that it is unreal.
Can this problem be solved. We search for truth, not illusion as we need to try to resolve this apparent dichotomy - either physical life is as we experience it or it is not.

Let us try to give some sort of explanation that, we hope, will enable some people at least to comprehend.
The God-force has created a number of bands of different frequencies, as we have previously explained.
Each frequency or carrier wave, is a basic structure, invisible of course, that enables life in its various configurations to exist.
We have previously compared these frequencies to the carrier waves that supply you with TV or radio programs. You change the carrier wave and you change the program.
This is an excellent way of explaining the various dimensions that exist, sometimes referred to as auras.
However, there is one major flaw in this analogy. TV and radio channels bring us illusion.
Even if the original information captured on cameras or on a microphone was of 'real' events, that which is broadcast to us is a sort of copy of the original event.

Even then, depending on our vantage point we would not necessarily observe exactly the same scene that the camera saw.
We would only see that which our eyes or ears could capture from that particular place.
Someone standing a few yards away would observe a slightly different version of the same scene. This would go on as people more and more remote from you watched the same scene but got different impressions than your version.
Thus it is if, say, a crime is committed and the police interrogate various people who claim to have witnessed the crime, they give slightly or startlingly different versions of what happened.
Then, of course, we have the vagueness of memory.
People describe the same person as wearing a black coat, a green coat a red coat. Of having blond hair, brown hair, black hair and so on.

The point we are trying to make is that no two people have exactly the same concept of an event.
This being so, how can we be sure of what physicality is?

Now, if we carry this thought on, we ask ourselves, what is the truth about life?
We accept that some people are male, some female.
Some with white skin, others with black, brown, yellow and so on.
Some people live in big houses, some in small.
We could go on endlessly describing the differences between any two people and any two situations.
And yet we all say that we live in a physical world.
A moment's thought will show that there is a problem.
How can physicality be real if no two people experience the same thing?
So, we need to search deeper to reveal just what physicality is.
Clearly it cannot be as solid as we imagine or we would all have some degree of common acceptance, some common denominator that would give us a basis for comprehension.

So, where does the idea of solidity, of physicality come from?
This is where this great illusion concept is born.
The archangelic beings that helped construct physicality - the Directors of Life (DOL) - needed to find a method of persuading us that planet Earth is solid and all life that is on it has solidity also.

So, they implanted in our minds a concept that is difficult to describe and difficult to comprehend.

They created in our collective Logos, not only that we are alive and that we are God but also the concept that, for the duration of an incarnation, the conviction that we are physical.

This is a very weak reply to the question so we will try to expand.

The DOL put, in association with our Logos, a concept that we could identify with the carrier wave that corresponds to physicality.

This concept allows us, from the moment of our incarnation until its termination, a belief that what we see and experience is real in terms of physicality.

The closest that we can get to explaining it is to ask you to imagine that you are watching a performance on TV but that you are not merely an observer but that you are actually one of the performers. That you are taking part in the program being revealed on the screen.

We have mentioned this before in other talks on the subject of reality but we have mentioned it again in an attempt to enable you to realize that physical reality is but an illusion.

However, you have no option but to accept this illusion as it is put into association with your Logos and thus is as important to you as the fact that you are alive and are God.

Thus, people incarnate have little or no choice but to accept that physicality is real - at least for the duration of their incarnation - and then we can move on to other forms of apparent physicality but in astral form with different rules to the game.

We will say as a last part of this explanation that it is possible to break through this illusion mentally and see life as an illusion but, even then, that very advanced person would still be bound by the fact that whilst in physicality he is bound - to a certain extent - by the rules of physicality.

That part of his Logos that ties him to physicality cannot be broken until his incarnation ends.

Thus all humans and all life on planet Earth has this lock that binds him to physicality.

To return to what we were discussing previously, the move from physicality to astral, at the end of our incarnation is possible because the lock mentioned above opens and frees us from being tied to physicality.

Once this happens, the person that is you is freed from the shackles of physicality and the person can move away from physicality and into the astral realms, permanently.

Some people, through meditation are able to move into their astral form for a while but are compelled, always, to return to the physical world.
This chain that binds us to physicality is seen by some mystics as a silver cord. It is the tie that binds us to our physical body during our incarnation.
Other people watching a dying person say that they see the 'light' leave the eyes of that person at the moment of their demise.
Once again, this is the animating spirit - the real person - leaving the body when the tie is broken.

Either way, the fact of the matter is that, once the cord is broken, once the lock is opened, the spirit of that person leaves its connection with its physical body and is liberated.
Before going on, let us spend a few moments in examining who 'you' are so that we may better understand which parts of you are freed and which parts remain with this corpse.
Now, we can't tell you every part of your spiritual body because it is far too complicated and complex for most people to understand and, although we wish to be open and honest with you, there is no point in confusing you. Indeed, there are many people who have spent long years in the heavenly realms who are still not advanced enough to understand what constitutes a human.

We are all familiar with the physical body that by some miraculous means has a heart that beats without us needing to pump it (except by those who have what is called an artificial heart), causing blood to circulate around the body and through the brain, the blood absorbing nutrients and particularly oxygen via the lungs that, in some way that people seldom question enable the brain to send electrical signals to the various parts of our body to keep it alive. Do people question what force causes the heart to beat, supplying the brain with what it needs to produce electrical signals that cause the heart to beat?
This almost equates to the chicken and egg situation that was mentioned a few chapters ago. The difference being that we know what keeps the whole system working.

The 'magic' that keeps the system functioning is that which we refer to as the 'spirit'.

Whilst this is so, the spirit - which is actually the God-force that we have mentioned many times - may well be the motor as in the motor of an automobile it is not the whole story by any means.

If you are familiar at all with the workings of an automobile, you will realize that to make that mechanical contraption take you anywhere, much more is required.

So, the spirit, being the power source of any living object, required many more things to make it function.

In the case of a human there are a large number of invisible spiritual parts that must work together to enable a person to be 'alive'.

We have already mentioned some of these; higher self (or higher mind), mind - closely associated with physical brain - imagination, will, auras, chakras and so on.

As we said, there are a number of other parts that we cannot, for the moment, describe because we do not wish to stray from the subject, all of which must work silently in the background in order for the physical body to operate.

These spiritual parts are locked together with the physical body and the Logos but, at the moment of death, the lock is opened and the spiritual attributes are free to wander away from the body.

We apologise for taking so long to get to the point of where what is referred to as the spirit goes to, once freed from the body, but the subject is complicated and we want you to have a clear understanding of what happens at the moment of death so we feel obligated to keep bringing in other aspects as they arise.

Once again we must break off to mention near death experiences (NDE).

It happens, for one reason or another, to some people that they appear to die and find themselves going through the death experience that we hope to describe shortly.

The point that we wish to discuss is that, sometimes, the person is met by what seems to be a god like figure and is told that it is not yet his time to remain in the heavenly spheres, and that he must return to his body and to his life on Earth.

The question we ask and hope to answer is, how does this god like figure know that the person is not truly 'dead'?

The answer, quite simply, is that the person who informs the victim that he is not truly dead is able to perceive the silver cord, the link between the physical body and the spirit in heaven and thus can be sure that the person might have his vital functions no longer working, but that the person is not truly dead. Once that cord is severed the person must be considered 'dead' and nothing can resurrect him.
So the person in heaven sees that there is still a connection between the soul and the body and advises the so called dead person to return to his body and he does.

So, at long last, let us examine what happens when we get to the sad, or happy, moment when this tie to physicality is broken and the spirit is, at last, free to reassume its long journey back to the Godhead.

Now, once again, as we have mentioned in various discussions on life after death, we must say that there are a number of ways that a spirit may be liberated from its ties to physicality.
In the most unfortunate case, a foetus may not reach full term and is aborted by accident or by design.
The term abortion has long been a bone of contention amongst religious people and is considered to be a form of murder by some.
We wish to reassure any prospective parents that, although we do not condone abortion, it is not murder.
Despite much debate as to the exact moment when a spirit (a soul) associates itself to the physical body of the embryo physical body, we wish to reassure all prospective parents that the spirit (Logos) actually makes contact with the baby at the moment of birth and at that moment the body springs to life, usually with a howl of protestation and everyone associated with that birth breaths a sigh of relief knowing that their child has safely been delivered.
However, from time to time the spirit cannot link with the foetus and withdraws in which case we say that a baby is 'stillborn'.

A baby's body, being very fragile can be subject to a number of accidents which can provoke the necessity for the spirit to withdraw and then we say that the baby has died.
Then, later in life, there are a number of illnesses or accidents that can cause an early demise of the person and lastly, there is old age which brings about an inevitable collapse of the link between body and spirit.

Although we feel rather guilty that we have taken so long to get to the point that we originally proposed talking about, we will, once again, break off to discuss just what 'old age' is.

A human person consists of two parts, the physical body and the spiritual elements.
The spiritual elements are immortal and are connected to the physical by this lock associated with the Logos that we have already mentioned.

Now the physical part grows and declines in two stages.
Up until the age of almost fifty years of age the various auras link with us one after another, typically, every seven years.
As there are seven auras, a person is not a complete human until he is approximately fifty years of age.
During this first fifty years of his life he is drawing energy into his physical body from the atoms in the atmosphere and also from the energy that is contained in what is termed 'dark matter'.
But all energy must be kept in balance and so, from that moment onwards, the energy that was drawn into the physical body must be returned to the cosmos.
Thus, as one passes the age of fifty, the physical body, returning the energy used to create his body during the first part of his incarnation, starts to grow physically weaker and we start to see signs of old age.
The hair on the head turns grey and does not grow so quickly.
The body is subject to illness increasingly and the body exhibits all the signs that are observed in elderly people.
This 'giving back' process continues until the person declines to the point where the body can no longer contain the spirit and the link between the spirit and body breaks and the spirit is released.

We wish you to comprehend that this is a hypothetical example and, although true in principle, the effects of this giving back of energy show marked variations.
No two people are the same so the speed with which one gives up the ghost varies from person to person as does one's resistance to illness, depending on that person, his lifestyle and so on.
But we have described why the physical body, sooner or later, becomes unable to contain the spirit and why a person dies of old age.

We would also like to mention that this chase after perpetual youth is pointless.
No quantity of rejuvenating creams spread over the body, no face lifting operations that some people feel compelled to undergo will hold onto youth.
The process of the body breaking down is inevitable and it is futile not to accept it.
It would be better that one grows old gracefully as do animals.
There can be beauty in age just as there is beauty in youth.
We would also like to stress the advantage there is in having all of the auras attached and thus, has more chance of making wise decisions instead of the rash, impulsive actions that young people often take.

Eventually, whether through accident, illness or age the cord snaps and liberates the spirit.
Generally speaking, the spirit, the true 'you' goes to heaven.
But there are a number of ways in which this journey to heaven can occur.

We will describe, first, the tunnel of light.
What happens in this instance is that within a very short space of time after the lock is opened and the spirit freed, the person finds himself in a long tube of multi-colored lights. He finds himself drifting slowly along this tube without having to walk. He moves automatically.
He may hear music of some sort.
This tunnel, this tube, is actually a portal that opens momentarily to convey the person to the next dimension.
This portal is actually an aura connected to a chakra point at the top of the head and actually exists all the time.
The person, when incarnate does not normally see either the chakra nor the aura but they are there and are part of his make-up, constantly maintaining a link between body and his higher self, higher mind which is also heaven.

So, the spirit, now freed from its physical body, is a being of light and is naturally drawn by the law of mutual attraction towards the light that it sees. This is, of course, the tunnel of light which is the chakra and aura that will conduct him back to his home - heaven.

As he progresses down this tunnel he will see a light, bright white, the light at the end of the tunnel.
When he arrives at this point he steps into a beautiful world.

Most people see this as a never ending and most beautiful park land. It is sometimes called 'Summerland'.
He will be greeted by a person, the likes of which he will never have met before.
This person will appear extremely bright and exudes total love.
Many people think that this person would be God, Jesus, Buddha or one of the great saints.
It isn't.
It is one of the many people in the heavenly realms that choose to spend their time helping newly deceased people to acclimatise themselves to life in the heavenly spheres.
In heaven, holiness is light, evil is lack of light.
As this person is holy, he exudes light and also exudes total love.
This light and love will be strange and somewhat disturbing to the newly arrived spirit, so he might find it somewhat overwhelming at first.

Now, we stop at this point in describing arrival into the afterlife in order to describe other means by which deceased persons can be taken to heaven.
It can and does frequently happen that a person approaches death slowly and over a period of time.
The angels who preoccupy themselves with assisting people to make the crossing make a decision to send a family member to greet the newly deceased person. This is to help make the crossing less dramatic.

In this case, the family member approaches, in the astral realms, the dying person, mixes with the auras of that person and waits patiently for the moment when the chain breaks and the person is released.
Then, as the person concerned leaves his body, often feeling completely bemused as to what is happening to him, he is greeted by the person who has come to help him cross over and is taken to the summer land.
One might ask why the tunnel of light does not appear?
The answer is that, with the sort of person who dies not knowing anything about spirituality and not having studied spirituality during his life, his auras would be weak and would take some time to form sufficiently to create a tunnel of sufficient strength to support the weight of the spirit of the person, there is always the danger that the spirit might wander about in the low realms and be attacked by negative entities, thus causing even more confusion.

To avoid this, a relative or a close friend greets the person and escorts him, by the law of mutual attraction back to heaven, from whence he came.

Now, we consider the case of sudden death due to accident or suicide.
The result would be similar to what is mentioned above.
For those who have been good and kind for most of their lives, they would have strengthened their auras even if they have not consciously done anything to strengthen them. That person would find himself in the tunnel of light - the head aura - and would proceed to the light of Summerland.
Similarly for someone who had done little to develop his auras, a person would immediately be dispatched to receive the deceased person and would guide him to heaven.

We must mention something that has only recently been developed.
There are a number of people who put out messages advising people that the tunnel of light is a trap and is created to enslave the dead and is part of an endless reincarnation event.
A moments thought will show that this is the total opposite to what should normally happen.

Fortunately, the number of people around the world who know of this idea is relatively small and so the vast majority of dead people see the tunnel of light and go into it and quickly find themselves in heaven and are met by a loved one to be escorted there.
But there are a small number of people who are convinced by this evil argument and resist the tunnel of light and resist to pleadings of their loved one offering to escort them to heaven.
As those who have read this book thus far will quickly realise, this recent idea is an Archon invention.
One should always be on the lookout for Archon intervention in our lives.
The Archons are constantly seeking to harm humanity.
It is easy to see Archon intervention.
Anything that one can feel is natural, good, beneficial and that one is told is harmful, is sure to be of Archon origins.
These entities do not invent but they take events that occur in life that are good and turn them upside down and present them as evil.
Evil things that one would normally reject, Archons present as good, beneficial and positive.

Thus, in the case of proceeding down the beautiful tunnel of light which would normally be accepted as a pleasurable experience, people are encouraged to reject.
As we all have free will, a small number of people, when they die, refuse this tunnel of light, refuse to be guided by a loved one and so thus find themselves in 'limbo'.

Limbo is not a place so much as a state of mind.
The person wanders about, close to Earth, completely lost and confused.
This, once again, creates fear which if food for Archons.
This state of being in limbo can last a short time until the person calls for help and an angel comes and guides him to summer land or it can last for long ages in the case of a person who refuses to believe he is dead.
He becomes what is known as an Earth-bound spirit.
These Earth-bound spirits are the cause of hauntings which are quite simply people deceased who refuse to believe that they are dead and thus remain, in spirit form, in their old homes.
Thus, when they see new people coming in to occupy what they consider to be their house, they seek to chase them away.

We who live in the heavenly realms cannot intervene as we have no right to interfere with free will but it saddens us to see people suffering either through ignorance or through the evil actions of others.

Once again we are concerned that the concept that the tunnel of light is a trap might become collective wisdom that most would believe, which is the objective of the Archons and those who work to spread their evil agendas.
Thus we urge all who can to refute this imbecility and encourage all to accept that the tunnel of light is the connection between man and heaven.

To round off this chapter on the dying process we should mention the etheric double.
As we have explained, all life has a physical body, seven auras and seven chakras.
Now, the auras can contain a great deal of power and, if they were to be directly connected to the human frame, could cause harm.
Thus, the chakras - which are the connecting points - are connected to an etheric double.

This appears as a grey mist surrounding a person. Its purpose is to act as a transformer reducing the power of the auras to a level acceptable to the human body.

It is not an aura, it is, in a way, part of the physical body and when a person dies, the etheric double will dissolve back into etheric matter from which it was made.

But it can wander about on its own for a while and is sometimes seen in graveyards as a misty white figure wandering near the place where someone was recently buried.

It will eventually dissolve and, if seen, should not be the cause of fear as it is not alive and will not harm anyone.

CHAPTER 10

INTO THE LIGHT

In the last chapter we described the dying process and how, once the lock is broken that chains us to our body, we usually, go to a light area called by some 'Summerland'.

This area appears very bright to most new arrivals for the simple reason that, for the first time since the person left heaven to descend into incarnation he is able to see clearly the world that surrounds him.
Planet Earth is a dark and dismal place for the simple reason that humans are tied to a physical body that is not made to see clearly. The term used to see clearly is a French word 'Clairvoyance'. There is no direct parallel to that word in the English language. Clair means to see clearly, voyance implies looking into the astral world. Thus to see clearly into the astral realms.
But, we would say that if someone had the ability to see planet Earth as she really is, that person would have a totally different experience. Planet Earth when clearly seen is a beautiful place but for many long ages man has been looking with eyes that are partially blind folded and thus appears dismal.
This is the result, not of genetic manipulation by the Archons exactly, but by their influence on humanity in their never ceasing attempts to create a dismal world so that they – the Archons – could benefit from the unhappiness created.
Fortunately, as we have stated, their domination over humanity is coming to a close and, gradually, people will start to see clearly again.

The reason that this was mentioned is because when a person's incarnation is finished and he moves to Summerland he is seeing life as it should be seen on Earth were it not for the Archon influence.
He arrives, usually, in a beautiful park area. Vast expanses of well kept lawns, miles of flower beds of lakes, of paths and benches and the overall effect is staggering for most people.
The air is filled with the perfume from the flowers and gentle music fills the air.
It is all an illusion, of course, just as planet Earth is an illusion but seems just as solid and real as planet Earth does.

The person is met, if he exists from the tunnel of light, by a very bright and holy looking person. This person, as we have already mentioned is someone who devotes his time to welcoming the new arrivals.

Now, we must mention a strange effect.
The new arrival will find himself alone for some time with this helper but a moment's thought should indicate that this is not logical.
There must be a number of people of all nationalities, races, skin colors etc, dying each moment from a variety of causes and thus one might expect that there would be a number of new arrivals also being greeted by angelic hosts but, no, the new arrival finds himself alone with the person sent to greet him.
Where are all the other people arriving in Summerland each moment?

We have to understand that heaven works by different rules, different laws than those that apply on Earth.
If Summerland was on Earth we would, no doubt, see a large number of new arrivals and a large number of people greeting them.
But the person is alone with his host who greeted him.
How is this possible?
The laws that heaven work under are spiritual laws. The first is "All is one and one is all."
The implication of this law allows us to create our own reality because we are one and that one is God. Therefore each person in heaven is able, through his imagination, to exercise his right to be the sole person in heaven.
Obviously, that statement seems ridiculous and will need to be explained but, for the moment, let us accept that the host, the person who comes to greet the newly deceased person creates, with his mind, the desire to be alone with the newly deceased person and so he creates a space where no one else exists, just him and the person stepping forth into the light.
Of course, all the other people preparing to greet a newly deceased person does the same so all who have recently died are alone with his host.

The host will appear radiant and shining, the result of his level of spirituality. Love, pure love, radiates from him as he waits patiently for the deceased person to approach him.

The host will explain that the person has left Earth forever, his cares and worries that had plagued him for all his incarnation are at an end, left behind with his body.
He explains many things and will answer any questions that the new arrival might have and reassure him that all is well.

This will happen to all people regardless of their life style and cause of death.
There is no judgement in heaven.
However, another spiritual law is the law of mutual attraction – like attracting like.
To use a Biblical term, "As ye sow, so shall ye reap".

This brings us to the life review.
At a certain point, when the newly arrived person is ready, he will have his life review. This life review all go through.
They see their incarnation, the good and the bad that they did, the mistakes that they made and the lessons they learned.
They will see the people they made happy and the people they hurt.
They will feel exactly the emotions of the people with whom they interacted.
The joy they spread and the unhappiness they caused.
This life review is a chance for the deceased person to step back from his life on Earth, see what his life plan was and to see how far he followed it.

This life review is important because, in heaven, we have no secrets. What we did while we were incarnate we can hide from others but not in heaven.
Spiritual progress must be based on honesty and openness and so the life review gives us the chance to appraise our level of spirituality.
From that review, a process starts that automatically draws us, via the law of mutual attraction, to the level of heaven commensurate with our level of spirituality.
So we suddenly find that this period of isolation with the host person changes and we find ourselves in the level of heaven that matches our spiritual level.

We find ourselves in the company of like minded people who welcome us into their midst.
Now, exactly where we go and where we find ourselves is difficult to describe, not because it is complicated to describe but because there are so many areas; literally thousands.

Just imagine here on Earth the countless points of views. It would be an endless task.
In a similar fashion, in heaven, for each and every point of view there is an area and in that area one finds discarnate people who think like the recently deceased person.

The advantage of this is that it avoids conflict. If everyone that you see share the same opinion on all matters, there cannot be conflict and discussion. Further, each group lives in his own isolated bubble of created reality so no one from an outside thought area could wander in.

However, from the point of view of us wandering about observing the different groups let us assume that we could enter these different bubbles of created reality and observe the groups living there. Imagine we could eavesdrop on their conversations.
What would we see and what would we hear?

We mentioned that there are countless groups all drawn to their various groups by the law of mutual attraction; like attracting like.
So, we would find people who feel most comfortable with others that think like them.
Thus, we find groups drawn together by race, color, religion, sex, political views and so on.
It must be said that none of those things have any significance once one leaves the Earth plane but we arrive in the heavenly spheres with exactly the same feelings and emotions that we had on Earth. Nothing changes.
Therefore it is amusing to study these diverse groups and listen to them earnestly discussing topics that have absolutely no relevance in heaven nor, it must be said, did they have any importance whilst in incarnation, only the importance that lost souls gave them.
These same groups go on believing in the importance of nonsensical topics but it gives them something to do.
They will grow out of that childishness one day and pick up the reigns of spiritual life.
In the meantime we leave them to their world of illusion.
So, to avoid discussing these countless groups and getting lost in the intricacies of their beliefs, let us just group them into 3 separate sections:
Those, spiritually advanced.

The vast majority that are not bad but have just lived a 'normal' life.
The evil ones.

As we said, the law of mutual attraction gathers like minded people together and places them in a part of heaven commensurate with their spiritual advancement.
Now, God is light.
So heaven contains various levels where the light is brighter or dimmer according to the levels of spirituality of the people attracted to those areas. The degree of light is created by the collective thoughts of the occupants of those areas.
So, at the very highest level, close to God, we would find a land of extreme beauty and beings of extreme beauty and brightness.
It must also be said that once humans arrive at that level they would have long outgrown the need for any form of physicality and they live as beings of light in a world of light. But for the sake of our trying to describe to you the various levels of heaven, let us assume that the beings of beauty live in a world of beauty.

Next let us examine the world of ordinary people. This group have passed their incarnation without trying to advance spiritually.
They may have paid lip service to a religion but their focus during their incarnation was work, family, TV, sports and so on – ordinary people. There is nothing wrong with this group and we do not criticize them. They did their best to look after their families and much of life depends on this, the working class.
However, their level of spirituality being less than the illuminated ones, they live in a world less bright.
This would resemble Summerland to a large extent.

In that area of heaven they would generally meet with various members of their family with whom that had an affinity and also some friends that they had on Earth that had passed to heaven before them.
We will also say that they may well be presented with pets they had whilst incarnate and with whom love had blossomed.
This obviously depends upon the ability of the animal to be able to experience love because some animals can generate this emotion whilst others have not yet developed it.

So, we would expect to see people walking about accompanied by pet dogs and, so a lesser degree, cats.
Occasionally one might see a person in the company of other animals of high order, felines, wolves and all sorts of bizarre pets but, of course, it is rare.

Now, we must explain that the law of mutual attraction is always at work drawing like to like.
This law works in two directions.
Thus a person might well find himself in the company of friends and loved ones but, equally, he would never encounter those that he neither cared for nor those that he had never met.
There are exceptions to this of course.
We are all watched over and guided by higher beings, so the recent visitor to heaven would, occasionally receive the visit from a more advanced person who will help him progress through the heavenly spheres.

We have described much of the Summerland area in the previous volume, "The Stairway To Freedom", so we do not propose to cover much about it here.
All the books that we hope will be published, given by us, link together and all should be read in order to obtain a complete understanding of physical and spiritual life.

So we will stop here in the description of where the average person finds himself and move, briefly, to an overview of the doleful areas known as hell.
Once again, we have covered, extensively, that area in the above-mentioned volume and refer the student to that work.

What we will explain is why a person should go to hell, although we are sure that we all agree that some deserve to suffer in the degree that they made others suffer.
However, we make it plain that one is never judged in heaven except by oneself.
The people who live in the heavenly spheres do so because they realize that it is pointless to judge another. Judgement plays no part in life outside of the physical plane.

But, there is a simple, but powerful, law that is always at work that makes sure that everyone is in their correct place.
We have mentioned this law many times.
It is the law of mutual attraction.
It has been given many names by a number of generations.
As ye sow, so shall ye reap being a famous one attributed to the master Jesus.
What it means is that everyone, during his incarnation decides to act in a certain fashion. Thus is his personality moulded.
When that person's incarnation is over, he will automatically be drawn by the law of mutual attraction to that area of the afterlife commensurate with his personality.
The life review explains to the person why he might find himself in a high or low area of heaven.
Thus, he cannot complain that he has been unfairly judged.
He understands that his actions during his Earthly incarnation draw him to the level that he finds himself.

We have to say that some people find it easy to repent their actions while others, filled with 'righteous indignation', think themselves hard done by and thus remain in the dismal spheres for long ages refusing to repent what they saw as a law filled life.
In this group we often find Judges and other law officers, religious leaders of many denominations and others who considered it their right and duty to judge, control and punish others.
This is the way that the law of mutual attraction works bringing happiness to love filled people and bringing misery to hate filled people.

But, the good news is even the most egocentric people usually realize that hate is pointless and so, sooner or later they repent and can then be assisted towards the light filled areas.

We wish, at this point, to make a statement that may shock many people who are convinced that heaven and hell are factual places to which one gravitates. In a way they are right because, either when one's incarnation ends, we are drawn to light or dark areas that appear just as real as Earth appears to those incarnate but those areas are illusion.
We have already mentioned that planet Earth and the incarnation experience is illusion.

In a likewise manner, heaven and hell are illusionary planes created by cosmic consciousness.
What actually happens is, at the end of an incarnation a person is drawn to a level of consciousness commensurate with that person's level of spirituality.

So, all the various levels of heaven/hell that exist are actually just levels of spiritual awareness.
However, to realize this, at the level that most people are at does not make much difference.
Just as it makes little difference to realize that incarnation is an illusion because we are all still tied to it by the silver cord whilst incarnate, to realize that the afterlife is an illusion makes no difference. The experience seems totally real and has to be experienced.
We mention that the planes of heaven and hell are part of the great illusion because we are obliged to talk about it whilst we are explaining the reality of life. But we all experience the heavenly and hellish planes as reality for long ages until we have developed sufficiently to be able to see through the illusion.

CHAPTER 11

THE WAY THROUGH THE LIGHT

In previous chapters we mentioned the path that the spirit takes once it is freed from the physical body.
In this chapter we will describe the path that is taken through the heavenly spheres as one settles into the spiritual life in the heavenly dimensions.
We have intimated that what is termed heaven is a series of illusions but, as one progresses through these areas they appear real just as an Earthly incarnation appears real.

We already gave an overview of Summerland and a brief glimpse into Heaven and Hell.
However, these areas that we looked at presumed that the people who stay in Summerland or Hell are those who are not far removed, spirituality, from those that have recently finished an incarnation on Earth and, thus, have only a limited spiritual development.

We intend to investigate the higher areas of the spiritual planes, talk about what they look like – as far as it is possible to describe them – and talk about the beings that live there.
So, when someone is ready to advance beyond the beautiful and peaceful Summerland, he starts to feel the desire to progress.
It must be said that a normally good person can reside in Summerland as long as he desires and some remain permanently in that area as it satisfies the yearnings of their soul, but many, eventually, start to feel the desire to progress.
So, unconsciously, they reach out with their thoughts and their thoughts are picked up by angelic beings charged with helping and monitoring the progress of people in all the various planes of both heaven and hell.
This, when they understand the desire of someone to progress, causes great delight to these angelic beings as they know another soul is on the path to perfection.
So, these angels meet together and study the past life of the individual; his life in heaven before incarnation, during his incarnation and what has interested him since returning to Summerland.

It must be noted that, upon the return of someone to Summerland, the individual is largely left to his own devices, allowing him to acclimatise, then either doing nothing but enjoying the peace and beauty of that place. Others are naturally drawn to investigate the mysteries of life as we have tried to present to you in our various talks and the questions that we have answered. But no one is pushed to study, any more than we push you to accept knowledge we present to you.
So, some people accept knowledge and some reject it.
Others are just not interested in progressing and so are left to live as they choose.

But, once someone feels the yearning to advance, experienced angelic beings examine the past history of that person, examine and quantify the knowledge that he has already accumulated and, above all, try to understand that person's interests.
It is extremely important to correctly identify a person's deep interests for, from the moment he leaves Summerland, he will follow a path that will take him along the long road to total knowledge of that subject.
Thus, eventually the person is approached and asked if he would be in agreement to follow a certain path for many long years.

We break off here to make a comparison between what occurs in Heaven and that which occurs on Earth.
A child is taught basic skills but, at some point decisions as to the future are made.
Some drop out of school and just drift.
Others continue with their studies until they feel the desire to specialize.
These specialities can cover a wide gamut of subjects but, if the student follows a path, he might well continue for all his career in that field.
So, you can see the similarity between behaviours in Heaven and on Earth.
As above, so below.

Therefore, you can also see the importance of choosing the correct road for the person because it would be futile to push someone into a discipline that did not interest him.
These disciplines, these paths can cover any subject imaginable.
It is often thought that the only subject taught in Heaven is spirituality.
This is not so, it is far from the truth.

Every conceivable subject is available for study and students are encouraged to experiment and develop new technologies and new ways of quantifying matter, this knowledge eventually being made available to man incarnate.
Therefore, a subject of interest to the person seeking advancement is decided upon and the person leaves Summerland.
Should anyone think that they also abandon their loved ones, let us quickly disabuse you of that idea.
Through the development of telepathy and clairvoyance – natural abilities in Heaven – people who care for each other are always in contact.
Our old friend the Law of Mutual Attraction assures that.

So, as we just said, the person leaves Summerland.
This is where is gets complicated to describe where the individual is taken.
Some, interested in the study of plants for instance would be taken to an area where a vast range of plants are growing.
There would also be laboratories where one can study the microbiological aspect of plants.
Further, there are areas where the DNA of plants is available for deep study.
So, the individual concerned would find everything that he would need to investigate and comprehend all that there is to know about plants.
Equally, there would be a number of students like himself learning.
These students would be of different levels of knowledge.
Some would be learning the different basic knowledge of biology and some would already be specializing in a particular aspect or, indeed, quantifying all that can be comprehended concerning one plant or one aspect of the life of a plant or plants.
You can see from these few lines that whatever aspect of biology of plants is known, that information is passed on to the student according to his interests.

The object of doing all this is not only for the benefit of the student but, eventually that knowledge is passed through the astral realms to people awaiting incarnation who have a natural interest in biology but also is passed to people incarnate.
This might be done through dreams or moments or "inspiration".
Thus, all of mankind, incarnate and discarnate, benefits from the studies of these students.

This concept is available to all people in Heaven that desire to progress whatever their interest.
No aspect of knowledge is ignored.
Whatever someone desires to study, there is an area, a school one might say, available for the student to study.
However, there are no examinations, no diplomas.
Each student continues his studies until he is satisfied that he has learned enough.

As time does not exist in Heaven, a student may study for as long or short a time as he desires.
Some stay for vast amounts of time studying a certain subject.
Of course, should the student realise that a mistake was made and he is not really interested in the designated subject, he may cease and choose another route.

So, we wish all students of cosmic consciousness to understand clearly that life in Heaven is not, in most cases, just a time spent in idleness.
Heaven is a hive of activity carried out in a very organized fashion so that all those who wish to be active can be and can follow whatever path interests them to whatever degree of perfection they seek.

For those who still feel the need for housing, it is provided and, in almost all cases, there are planes of beauty very much like Summerland and depending on the degree of spiritual advancement of the individual as he progresses through the spheres, light becomes brighter and everything shines more.

The exception, of course, would be for those brave souls who decide to experience the doleful areas referred to as Hell, because there are a number of people who undertake to devote their future to trying to help the wretches suffering in Hell through their past misdeeds committed when incarnate.

We have great admiration for those people that we could refer to as nurses, doctors, psychologists and social workers, who devote vast amounts of time delving into the doleful planes of Hell instead of choosing a different path enabling them to stay in the light and beauty.
So, these helpers go down into the stygian depths of Hell where the most terrible criminals, if we may refer to them in that Earthly term, reside.

The people who reside in those depths of darkness and despair do so because, when they were incarnate they committed the most heinous crimes against man and animals. They did these crimes for the pleasure of administering suffering.
The sheer pleasure of inflicting excruciating pain on any creature capable of undergoing that torture.
When these people had their life review they showed no signs of remorse and so, by the Law of Mutual Attraction, were drawn to levels where they, too, could experience suffering. Not physical, but mental suffering.

So, these social workers descend from time to time down to the depths in which these terrible people reside and try to persuade them to repent their crimes so that they could start the long climb back towards the light.
Generally speaking that help is refused. The people are so far removed from any human decency that they are incapable of accepting help and advice and, although most of them are deeply unhappy, they prefer to remain where that are rather than change.
This may seem odd to ordinary people that anyone would wish to live in the depths of Hell rather than accept help to escape but, there are such people. Many of us have met people with a similar attitude.

We break off here in our description of the residents of the darkest areas to question an alternative version of Hell believed to exist by many.
This is the fiery pit.
People describe in NDE's going down into a pit full of fire with imps torturing the victims and so on.
This dreadful place is described in the Bible in some detail and yet does not at all correspond with the Hell that we describe – dark, dank and dismal.
So, what is going on here that has created two places, one the opposite of the other?

Let us try to explain.
We have stated in other talks that thoughts are things and if enough people believe something to be true, it creates in the etheric realms, a thought form that appears real.

So, the Archons, many thousands of years ago decided to introduce the concept of a fiery pit.

The reason was that religions were first introduced in what we now call the middle east.

These are hot countries and before any form of modern air conditioning was introduced – a modern invention – people suffered from the heat. Therefore, it seemed logical to the Archons to introduce into their invented religions the concept of a fiery pit as a punishment as suffering from heat was all too well known.

Over the years, people started to believe in this place and so, in the low etheric realm, this place was created as a thought form.

Thus, when some Christian or Muslim people have a NDE and know that they have been less than good people, they find themselves in this fiery pit. It is not real, it is imagination brought into a type of reality.

To return to what we were discussing.

The depths of Hell.

It might be questioned why Hell exists at all and why it exists in ever more cold, dark and dismal realms?

The answer, as always is simple.

People have consciousness. There are endless aspects of consciousness.

Imagine, for example what it would be like if we could link with a being like the master Jesus and if we could savour what his consciousness would be like. Would it feel dismal and dark, mean, selfish, full of hate or would it feel the opposite to all that?

Would we feel joy, bliss, lovingness to all things?

We don't even need to answer that question because we all know the answer. So, being full of God's love for all, Jesus when his incarnation on Earth was finished, created in his new world in Heaven a space that corresponded to all those noble sentiments. We create our own reality in heaven much as we do whilst incarnate, but incarnation in this dense reality makes manipulation of reality more difficult. In the heavenly spheres, manifestation is instantaneous and so, when Jesus arrived in Heaven, his beautiful world in which he lives was already awaiting him.

It is the same for all of us. We create the reality we are drawn to according to our level of consciousness.

Thus, with regard to the various levels of Hell, the consciousness of numerous people is less than holy.

It ranges from just being selfish and not caring about other people at the highest end to the most cruel, psychopathic people imaginable at the extreme low end.

And so, just as Jesus created a paradise due to his extremely elevated consciousness, the lesser people create a place in Hell for themselves due to their negative attitudes. These areas are dark, dank and dismal areas because, if we could link with their consciousness, those would be the impressions that we would receive. The coldness and the darkness caused by shutting out the light of God.

So, for every aspect of consciousness both positive and negative there is a level of Heaven and Hell.

We now mention something that could not exist on Earth and it is this:
We mentioned that if we choose, we can go to places where we can learn and that, in those places, there is a variety of students and teachers.

Each one of these people would be at a particular level of consciousness and yet, they would all be mixing together.

The strange thing is that each one of these people would have associated with him his world created by his consciousness.

So, many people can mix and work together and yet each one has his individual reality, spirituality, associated with him.

We mentioned, that this could not exist on Earth and, in the obvious fashion that it manifests itself in Heaven it is so, but in fact, even on Earth people mix who are at various levels of spirituality but it is not obvious as it is in heaven. In Heaven it manifests itself also by the degree of light emitting from the astral body of the person.

We return once more into Hell and follow the noble spirits that undertake that work.

Those people would shine with the light of God emanating from their bodies and we could easily see that this would create a problem.

The individuals living for long years in the relative or total darkness would not welcome into their midst someone aglow with spiritual light and so, those that administer to the lost souls learn to lower their spiritual frequency so that they shine less brightly.

Thus, they are able to minister to those suffering in the darkness of Hell without frightening them.

This ability to lesson one's level of spirituality is an extremely difficult thing to learn to do as it flies in the face of their natural level of consciousness.
In fact, it causes these helpers extreme discomfort because they actually have to learn to be cold hearted entities like the people to whom they administer and we must admire such people who deliberately choose to become heartless wretches in order to be at one with the people they help.
Of course, when they leave Hell, they can shake off their low feelings and return to the noble beings they really are.

To complete this short overview of Hell, and why people are drawn there we should say that it happens from time to time that a person is not only not able to progress towards the light but he becomes more and more unlike anything that one could call an aspect of God that his God spirit becomes extinct. The light of God is snuffed out and the individual ceases to exist. Fortunately, this is rare, but is something that we have to mention.

The next part that we have to mention is how one progresses up through the spheres, the dimensions within the dimensions on the long progression towards perfection.
This is surprisingly simple in principle but, like so much to do with spirituality is the opposite to what one might imagine to be the case.
Logic would suggest that it would be a case of learning endless subjects, each one more difficult than the previous where as, in fact, it is the relatively simple task of letting go of ego.
Ego, as we have often said, is both part of the fight / flight protective aspect which, of course, we take into Heaven with us but is no longer needed in those peaceful, loving spheres as there is nothing to fight or to fear in the light filled domains, but ego is also that aspect of personality that gives us individuality – makes us feel separate, one from another.

At the risk of repeating that which we have already explained, the sense of individuality is actually our God aspect pushing us to be the unique recipient of God. It is given to us by God and is a vitally necessary part of us particularly when in incarnation.
We have mentioned that we see it clearly in the vegetable and floral community where a plant or a tree, for instance, does all that it can to be the dominant life force where it grows, seeking to get all the nutrients, moisture and sunlight that it requires to allow it to grow and be the best possible

example of God in incarnation at the expense of any and all other plants in its immediate area.

This is understandable of course. Otherwise, the God force could not be the ultimate power that it is. God gains experience through growth. God would not gain much experience from plants that remained weak and spindly, although it must be said that God is interested in all aspects of life, even failures. But, if a species died out, obviously, there would be nothing for God to learn from.

So, God pushes plants to grow to perfection even at the expense of robbing other plants of the energy they require.

Thus, there is a constant battle waging between plants to try to succeed at all costs.

This concept of trying to win the battle for life is part of the ego.

Now, we mention this because we retain this aspect of ego when we return to the heavenly spheres and it is very necessary to retain it as it gives us the drive to learn, to progress through the spheres in our drive to reach perfection.

Just as each plant on Earth strives to become the best possible example of its species, so we humans strive to be the best possible example of humanity in what ever field of activity we choose to pursue.

Once again, we stress that God can learn from failure but learns more from success.

So, man arrives in Heaven with at least two aspects of ego in place; fight / flight and the desire to succeed at the expense of all other humans.

It is obvious that the fight / flight aspect is quickly eliminated because it is not required outside of physicality and thus that aspect of ego dies from lack of nourishment.

But the drive to succeed remains and, we repeat, is placed within us by God itself to enable us to succeed in whatever domain we choose to explore, both during our incarnation and on into the endless non-physical spheres.

This ego driven desire to succeed at the expense of others flies in the face of statements that we have made earlier that we are all one.

We cannot be the unique holder of the God spirit, excluding all others and be at one with all life at the same time – or can we?

Is it possible to be the unique holder of the God Force and yet be part of and the total of all that exists at once?

We need to resolve this dilemma, this dichotomy of apparently being two opposing forces at the same time.

This is what we were referring to in this section of this chapter, exploring how we progress towards perfection by letting go of ego.

It occurs to us as we mull this problem over in our mind that we need to start by resolving one part first and then, hopefully, the second part will resolve itself.

Most of us find it easier to grasp the concept that we are all one. As we fill our lives with peace and as we develop love for all things we develop this ability to feel love and togetherness for all life.
So, we breath a sigh of relief; that is the first part resolved.
Then we turn our attention to the second part; getting rid of the feeling that we are the unique representation that matters of the God force.

Suddenly, God – our Higher Self – kicks in and protests. God itself, which is manifest in our Higher Self, refuses to take a back seat because it reasons that God is all that exists and God has chosen me to be its unique important person, as regards humanity at least. So, we sit down and try to resolve this problem.

We can concede that all humanity, indeed all life has the right to live, but we are not willing to let that kindness to others extend to the point that they are all that matters and I do not count at all. In other words, I demand the right to exist because God told me, via my Higher Self, that I was specially chosen by God to represent him (it).

Now, this is the great blockage to progress that we mentioned earlier and that all must resolve if they wish to progress towards the higher spheres.
It is not only rejecting ego, but entails, possibly rejecting God itself.

But, can we do this?
Rejecting ego is difficult enough for many people, and it must be said that a lot of people stumble at this hurdle and turn back, remaining permanently in the lower spheres of light, unable to reject ego completely.

But for those that do manage to pass this barrier, a yet much higher, more difficult barrier remains to be confronted.
What do we do about being the sole aspect of God in existence?

At this point, once again many turn back because to go on will take the person into uncharted waters.
This is understandable. Not everyone has sufficient blind faith to take the next step.
This step is to cut our connection with God – our Higher Self. We might think that we only have had our Higher Self for a relatively short period of time but, in fact, we have had the God spirit attached to us, constantly guiding and advising us for an enormous period of time and it is unthinkable for many to break that connection. Thus, progress halts at that point.

For those courageous enough to continue, they make the decision to reject their Higher Self not knowing where they might go and what might happen.

We can describe the process of excluding God from our lives and we can describe the destiny of those who take the plunge and see the processes through to the end but, nothing can describe the feeling of helplessness that this journey provokes. It has to be experienced in order to understand.

Surprisingly, this voyage into nothingness is quite well known.
It is mentioned in the Bible in connection with Jesus where it suggests that the master, before ascending into paradise, went to Hell.
It has been mentioned by people who have had a difficult problem to resolve and think that they have wandered through the wilderness but, of course, it was not so.

So, let us describe, as best we can, how this process unfolds.
Once the decision has been taken to reject the God aspect, a specially trained guide appears. Indeed, there might be more than one guide but this voyage into the unknown is not something that a person enters into lightly and so, much explanation, much study is required to prepare the student for the experience. If someone attempted to start the journey without sufficient preparation, it would end in failure.

Already, no one is permitted to attempt this journey unless they have been in the spirit world for sufficient length of time as to be in the possession of much spiritual education.
Equally, the person has to have sufficient strength of character to be permitted to face this ultimate test and has to have risen to sufficient heights to have the courage and faith to confront this challenge.

But, if it is decided that this person has sufficient attributes to face this test, he undergoes long and detailed training.
This test, if the person passes, is the ultimate one that will open the door to someone becoming an angel so you can see the importance of preparation in all aspects for passing.

Once the person passes this test, which we repeat, is challenging beyond anything that we can imagine, a sudden change occurs.
It is like a death and rebirth into a dimension that is excluded from all who have not passed this test.
This individual loses all sense of his individuality and becomes filled with the feeling of oneness for all life.
In effect, he becomes filled with God Power and becomes what is termed an Archangel.
His life is not finished at this point by any means, but his progress through the spheres in effect ceases as there are no more steps for him to take.
He becomes, in effect, a universe wide consciousness and he is able to send love to all people in all dimensions.
He becomes supremely happy, filled with God's power.
So, in effect, the story of man's progression from creation to ultimate God manifestation is complete.